Keyboard and pen.

*A pot-pourri of articles
and drawings by
Geoff Waterhouse*

--

Forheleneemilybeckyrubyellenandgeorge.

"Merry Christmas lads, sorry it's bloody Dodo again — but better make the most of this one..."

Introduction

Some of these little articles are from the pages of Cumbria Magazine, Lancashire Life and The Oldie Magazine. I'd like to thank the editors for allowing me their valuable space and giving me the confidence to continue my little jottings. My cartoons have appeared in several leading magazines such as Punch, Readers Digest, Saga and The Oldie and after some fifty years of trying even managed to grace the pages of Private Eye but this little compilation is more to do with my keyboard rather than my pen.

That being said, a sports magazine editor once told me he liked my cartoons because they helped to fill spaces in his magazine. Bearing this rather unflattering remark in mind, if I find a large space in this little book I may well fill it with a cartoon.

From these articles, you will detect a distinct Northern flavour. It's not all cloth caps and clogs – though they are both here, but don't let that put you off. I write and draw for pleasure (and the odd cheque) – hopefully this will be detected and enjoyed.

There are pieces of general interest and I'd be surprised if there isn't something you hadn't come across. Did you know for example that there was a WW2 German U Boat named after the Laughing Cow cheese or that there were originally over sixty factories in Lakeland making bobbins?

—

The Norse West Corner

I'm surrounded by Thwaites. One of my immediate neighbours is Satterthwaite and the other a Haythornethwaite. I've worked with a Cornthwaite and a Thistlethwaite (her first name was Heather) and I've known Braithwaites, Crossthwaites and Laithwaites. There are Garthwaites, and Gawthwaites, Applethwaites, Rossthwaites, Laythwaites, Subberthwaites and Stonethwaites, Cowperthwaites, Hebblethwaites and plain old Thwaites. I could continue with my thwaiting list - but it does go on a bit.

What links all these names is that Thwaite is derived from *thveit* a Viking word for a clearing. That doesn't mean that all those Thwaites have Viking ancestors, though some may have of course. Take old Postlethwaite in the accounts department. He isn't necessarily the great, great, great, grandson of 'Postlethwaite-the-Pillager', probably the only Scandinavian thing coursing through his veins is half a Carlsberg. His ancestors may well have had a 'Thwaite' tagged on to their names at some point in history simply because they were living in a 'Thwaite ' area.

If you are a Thwaite reading this, then I'm almost positive that one of your forebears was Olaf the Magnificent. I can visualise him now, a handsome figure standing 6 ft 4 ins with flowing blond hair cascading from an ornate helmet which sports golden wings. On the other hand he could have been Sven the swine heard who stood 4 ft high and 3 ft wide, slept with his pigs and never washed.

I've come across so many Thwaites because Lakeland was a natural centre for Viking settlement. Cumbria at the time was in the hands of the Angles, following on from the Celts. The Angles had settled the rich farmlands of the coastal plains, but the Vikings preferred the wooded hills and valleys with pastureland.

These new Viking settlers had sailed in from Ireland, Iceland and the Isle of Man and for the most part were converted Christians, quite compatible with the Angles, though the close proximity of two groups of Christians doesn't sound like a recipe for harmony to me !

When you think of Vikings you naturally associate them with rape and pillage and all that rather unsavoury side to their history,which did go on but not to the extent we are led to believe. They had what you might call, 'a bad press' beginning with the chronicles of the Lindisfarne monks, who had a particularly nasty experience at the hand of their Scandinavian guests in the year of their Lord AD 793.

There was another side to Viking culture. They were incredibly intrepid explorers. Their longboats sailed the

Mediterranean and others even reach North America. They were also traders and craftsmen with wonderful skills, but mainly they were settlers. That leads me back to the Thwaites, or at least to the original *thveit*.

There are numerous Viking settlements in the Lake District. This not only accounts for the the prolific number of place names with an Old Norse root, but also for words in the current local language. The hills in the North are called fells, from the Norse *fjall*, small lakes are known as tarns, from *tjorn* and streams are becks, from *bekkr*. Waterfalls in Lakeland are called forces, from the Norse *foss*, and a ravine is a gill or ghill from *gil*. A knott, describing a craggy feature on a fell, comes from *knutr*.

The list of Viking derived place names is incredible. Lots of 'Thwaity' ones of course, such as Esthwaite, Tilberthwaite, Haverthwaite Seathwaite and Burnthwaite. There's Bassenthwaite, Finsthwaite, Smallthwaite and Thornythwaite or Bleathwaite. Brackenthwaite and Waberthwaite as well as Beanthwaite (you think I'm making these up don't you). Ickenthwaite or Nibthwaite and even Thwaite Yeat. And there's more where they came from.

Swinsdale derives from the Norse word for swine, *svina -* and *dalr*, dale. Grizedale is from *griss*, the word for pig. Ennerdale was originally 'Einarr's Dalr, and Haweswater, 'Hoefer's'.

Most of these words and names are familiar to me since I've been brought up with them. I realised only recently, following a visit from a friend from Bristol, that they form a kind of 'Lakeland-speak'. It was his family's first visit to the Lake District and he found words such as Fell, beck, tarn and gill quite strange.

There are several places where you can discover examples of Viking sculpture, mostly in churches. The church of St Mary at Gosforth has some notable sculpture including a large cross in the church yard. It has been suggested that the beams of the small church of St Olaf at Wasdale Head are from a Viking longboat, though others dismiss this as a romantic notion. As the Vikings built mainly with wood it is not surprising that little evidence of their skills remains. Their legacy is mainly to be found in our language -as well as the genes in all (well some) of those Thwaites.

If some day you find yourself on a *fjall* walking trip in the Lakes and you are following a babbling bekkr, picking your way up a deep *gil* to picnic by a *foss* - think of old Postlethwaite in Accounts. Maybe, just maybe, one of his ancestors has been there before you.

I. To be healthy and strong you must make it a rule to go to the closet once every day, whether you think that you need to or not. You should go at the same time each day. The best time is after breakfast.

II. If you have to go to the closet more than twice in one day you have diarrhœa, and you should tell the Doctor at once.

III. If you pass two whole days without doing anything when you go to the closet, you should go to the sickroom for some Opening Medicine.

IV. If you swallow your food without chewing it, you are sure to have pains and make yourself ill and irregular.

V. Only the paper supplied is to be used.

VI. You should never be shy of speaking frankly to the Doctor about anything which you think is wrong with you.

VII. Remember that you are never quite hidden from other people's view here, and that to play any tricks with your body is frightfully dangerous; and will most certainly wreck your whole life. It does not in the least matter whether anyone sees you or not, as you cannot cheat Nature.

VIII. Remember that only beastly cads write anything whatever on the walls or doors of closets, or play any games there, or stand on the seats. Any boy caught doing so will be flogged. If anything is written up and the boy who wrote it cannot be found, a half-holiday will be stopped for the whole school.

IX. Boys who are really modest and decent will not use these places for conversation; nor will they at any time say things which they would not like their mothers to hear.

X. A boy with a dirty mind never has a healthy body, and is always a miserable weak beast, rotten at games and work.

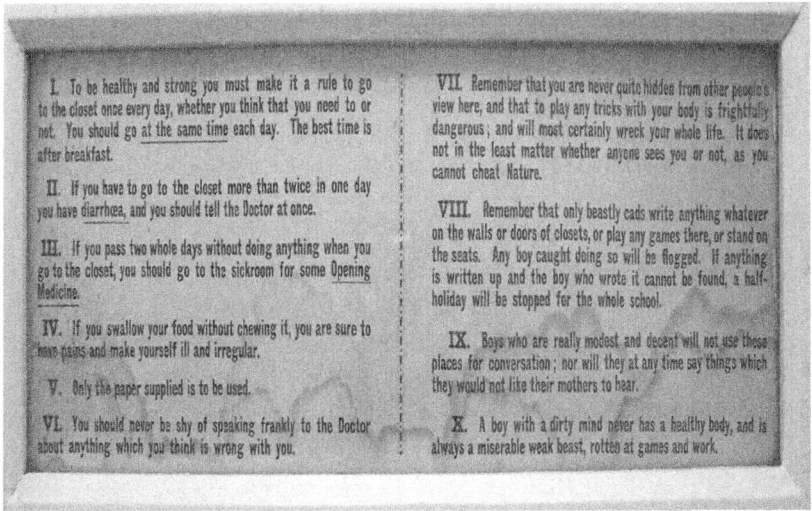

Beastly cads and Big Brother

The doom laden little notice reproduced here is possibly the forerunner of CCTV. For the early decades of the 20th century this was Big Brother, lurking in the lavatories of boarding schools watching out for the activities of beastly cads. This particular, suspiciously stained example, was rescued from a friend's old prep school and auctioned off, following what must have been a rather overdue re-vamp of the schools toilets. It now hangs in his downstairs loo keeping a vigilant eye on his guests' activities.

I've no doubt many public school readers will recall bizarre notices such as this. The rest of us, though not having the benefit of private education, were well acquainted with boarding school life and language. We had glimpses of this world through the literature of the era aimed at boys. Even comic heroes such as Billy Bunter lived in a world populated by *cads, chums, rotters* and *bounders*. They wandered through the *quads* and *dorms*, were *flogged* as *fags* and were *gated* for minor misdemeanours. My image of these schools may well be a little distorted but I was always quite envious of the imagined lifestyle.

It would appear however, that regardless of our backgrounds we boys were all potentially miserable weak beasts and apparently, risked being rotten at games and work. What we may have all been up to was frightfully dangerous and could most certainly have wrecked our whole lives. It's a tragedy when I imagine what I could have achieved in life if I hadn't played tricks with my body and cheated nature.

Amusing as this all is, it's not difficult to see how such Big Brother notices came into being. For the headmaster, controlling several hundred boys in a boarding school must have posed real problems. Boys will be boys, as they say, but what I read from the pen of Stephen Fry and others, playing tricks with their bodies seems to not just have been a normal part of life – but an obsession. How he survived to be a success is a minor miracle.

The other main concern of our closet all seeing eye was that of bodily functions, with an emphasis on regularity. A regularity, which was governed by the clock. In those pre and post war days, regardless of your school, the normal slippery, sharp edged toilet paper was enough to make anyone resist going to the toilet. Why the author of this notice insisted that 'only the paper supplied' should be used, makes you wonder what the boys had been using in its place. Perhaps blotting paper was considered superior in texture and absorbency and reams of the commodity were being smuggled from the classrooms – putting a strain on the school budget, not to mention the plumbing system.

Here again, I do have some sympathy with the headmaster. He was obliged to look after the education and welfare of the boys in his charge, It would be difficult to have kept a school running smoothly, if the whole school was constantly running - to the closet or being continually administered Opening Medicine. This would have also increased the matron and caretaker's workload. Could it be that our little notice was stained by the result of some traumatic, explosive cure for constipation? It is more probable, that its condition was due to a not uncommon competition, to see which boy could pee the highest, and our ever-watchful notice being the well-deserved target.

But what of my friend? He must have been a model schoolboy. He's a very successful fellow and jolly good at games. A credit to his school in fact. He does recall that as a new boy, he knew there was something he shouldn't be doing – but not actually knowing what it was. At my own school, it never occurred to me that someone was possibly watching me in the toilet. I thought privacy in the privy was written in the constitution. What a nightmare. All those frightfully dangerous body tricks and nature cheating activities would have been suppressed and I could have emerged as a disturbed adult.

It's catch twenty-two – in the loo.

water howse -

Bring me sunshine.

Eric Morecambe's bronze edifice erected on the
refurbished Morecambe promenade is rapidly becoming
one of the most photographed statues in Britain. It depicts
Eric doing his distinctive 'Bring me Sunshine' dance –
hopefully to bring sunshine to his hometown. Every few
minutes the cries of the circling seagulls are interrupted by
yet another group of visitors singing 'Bring me Sunshine' as
they emulate Eric's skipping pose for the family album.
The holiday town of Morecambe has suffered steady
decline and decay over the last few years as it tried to keep
up with its big sister Blackpool, just down the coast, with its
own brand of illuminations and unsuccessful theme parks.
Meanwhile, big sister Blackpool is shooting itself in the
foot, alienating itself from its core 'family holiday' business
by becoming the capital of the stag and hen party world

who stagger rowdily about the increasingly down market town.

HEYSHAM BOAT IN
MORECAMBE BAY
by Norman Wilkinson

A postcard from Morecambe's golden age.

Morecambe was always a smaller affair. A few good runs with a bulldozer could remove the motley selection of sea front eyesores and make way for apartments and hotels that would offer some of the best views in the country across Morecambe Bay. As a holiday base, it's just minutes away from the Forest of Bowland, Lancaster, Silverdale, Arnside and the Lakes, giving it a real chance to survive.

After years of dereliction and disrepair, the town's wonderful Art Deco Hotel, The Midland, had a face-lift. I think Morecambe has at last discovered that by refurbishing the promenade with a delightful stone jetty and a simple statue, its future lies with its actual location, and the more leisurely pursuits of the grey pound as well as a family holiday destination.

Long before Morecambe even existed, the Bay offered a

coach route for the intrepid, across the sands from Lancaster to Ulverston and beyond. Even up to the mid 19ᵗʰ century you could travel from Lancaster across the bay by coach and horses, described by the operators as an 'expeditious crossing'. These treacherous sands have been known to swallow up both coach and a full team of horses. Today it's more likely to swallow up a careless tractor servicing the cockle pickers - or the unfortunate pickers themselves It is said that the tide here races in faster than a galloping horse, which was bad news for the horse – but worse for the occupants of the coach.

Walks are organised on a regular basis across the bay under the guidance of the official, impressively titled Queen's Guide. There are unofficial guides as well and I don't think any of them have lost a client – yet. Actually, the walk across Morecambe Bay doesn't start from Morecambe. They are usually organised by charity organisations and involve all age groups from children through to t elderly folk, so you couldn't cross it at its widest point otherwise you'd lose hundreds of walkers in the process. They generally set off from the little town of Arnside and across to Kents Bank near Grange-over-Sands.

The tide at Arnside rushes in so fast that a hooter is sounded to warn visitors to vacate the beach. Changes to tidal flows and decades of indecision have seen the sands at Grange become a vast mud flat which has been colonised by a very virulent Sparta grass to the point where it could well be re-named Grange-over-Grass. It is still a very attractive little Victorian resort and the loss of its sandy beach has probably saved it from becoming a mini Blackpool with all the accompanying horrors. Hopefully, Morecambe will take note and opt for a similar marketing strategy of charm for its survival.

The walk across the bay involves a large helping of theatre. The guide meanders his flock of some hundred eager visitors, doubling the actual A to B distance, with the threat that should you stray from the route you will be swallowed up by the sinking sands. All rather dramatic of course, but a great day out, a bit like a coach trip – without the coach. The view from the centre is impressive even though it's not the real centre of the bay but a flat panorama of sand in all directions, with the mountains of Lakeland as a backdrop to the North, and over to the Pennines in the East.

Perhaps a few lighter, more portable resin casts of Eric could be made to mark the day's route across the bay. Visitors could then skip across singing - 'Bring me sunshine'. They could also sink a few 'half Erics' up to their chests with one arm outstretched declaring danger zones.

His 'Bring me Sunshine' dance could be a ray of economic hope to the town.

To bee or not to bee?

That was the question my late father had to consider following his collapse from an anaphylactic shock brought on by bee stings. The question was posed by our local Doctor who had just saved his life by swiftly administering an injection of adrenalin, and by my mother who had reached the end of her tether with his bee keeping activities. I'm going back in time here, wartime in fact, when I was just an infant. I don't recall the incident, but I do recall his bees. Actually, had it been today, he would have died. Back then, the village Doctor was round at the house in minutes. Try getting one round today.

The Doctor returned while he was recovering, armed with a large book on various traumas and read him a passage concerning snakebites. He ended with the words – 'and death ensues'. Something of a 'no-brainer' really, bees or death.

He kept two lots of beehives, two in the garden and others

with his beekeeping friends on the fells – for heather honey. The garden was always full of bees, they were everywhere. My mother complained that every time she brought her washing in, she brought a load of bees in with it. Ironing was a nightmare. I was constantly being stung, but mostly by bees I had upset with a fishing net or a stick in the hive. I can't really blame the bees – but mother did. Bad enough being buzzed outside and inside, but having her offspring attacked was a buzz too far.

Beekeeping, I have to say, is a fascinating hobby. Bees are capable of all manner of mind-boggling behaviour and communication skills. You probably know about their dancing technique for indicating the direction of a pollen source, but did you know that they can regulate the temperature inside their hive by controlling the air flow via unified wing power. Small creatures entering the hive can be stung to death, and then coated in wax to eliminate contamination. I can't claim to have seen this, but I can certainly verify their dislike of intruders – and their organised response.

Strangely enough, I never took it up myself, even though I'd been brought up with them. My father had all the beekeeper's paraphernalia; the trilby with a net attached, special gloves and a smoke box to puff smoke into the hive when you go about your hive maintenance business. The problem was, half the time he never used it all. I would watch him bending over the hive with bare arms and hatless, extracting a honey comb frame and the place would be alive with bees, I can hear them now, angry bees which send a simple message to me – at least put your hat and gloves on!

There were not many folk who kept bees in the village. So

dad was listed at the local Police Station as the man to call with regard to bee problems, if there had been a swarm spotted in the locality. Off dad would trot with a basket or a box to collect them. A swarm is an amazing sight, and even though bees don't really bother me, I don't think I would be brave enough to try and get all my bees into one basket.

If dad was listed in the emergency services as Bee Man – there was another chap down the road who became the original Spider Man. His hobby concerned spiders, snakes, lizards – anything exotic and creepy. His garden shed and garage was a mini menagerie. Preston Dock was the main port for Fyfes Banana boats. In the late forties and fifties bananas would be delivered to the local shops virtually direct from the port in long wooden boxes. Any creature that had stowed away in a bunch in the West Indies would often emerge in the greengrocers. Not just spiders, there would be all manner of giant insects and snakes. Fortunately, Spider Man was on hand.

By trade my father was an engineer and these skills were put to good use when he created his own Heath Robinson version of a honey extractor. Basically, it is extracted by centrifugal force. The comb frames are spun in a drum and the honey is forced out to the sides and collects at the bottom. My dad's version was created from a mini galvanized dustbin, and the power source was a converted, foot operated Singer sewing machine. A masterpiece of ingenuity. He would sit at his machine treadling away with wheels and belts spinning until the task was completed. Rows of jars of golden honey were always a feature in our kitchen. In wartime and post war Britain jars of honey were a great bargaining commodity too. These activities probably placated my mother for a time, - until the next bee attack.

Cock and Bull stories.

I was watching the TV programme 'Flog it' when a refined, elderly lady presented one of the show's experts, Jeremy Lewis, with a rather rustic looking walking cane. Inspecting it with a half smile and a twinkle in his eye, Jeremy asked if she knew what it was. She shook her head. 'It's a bull's pizzle', he explained, and added by way of clarification, 'a bull's penis'.

Apparently, following a lifetime of 'service' to the dairy or beef industry, the bull's penis can often enjoy another career in service as a walking cane. Having firstly been dried, sterilized and prepared by a taxidermist it then has a metal rod inserted along its remarkable 36" (or more) length to keep its erect status in permanent employment. I can vouch for this rather surprising dimension as I once witness an alarming spectacle when I was about six years old whilst playing in the barn of our local farm. From my vantage point overlooking the farmyard, the farmer and a couple of his farm labourers were coaxing the farm's bull to mate with a cow. When I use the term 'coaxing' I should really say guiding. The bull knew exactly what to do but it was a ferocious beast and need careful handling. Obviously, unlike the bull, I didn't have a clue what the whole performance was all about, but the length of the bull's appendage is an image that has remained with me for some seventy years.

The 'pizzle' is an Old English word for penis and apart from servicing cows and being transformed into walking canes it has the potential other uses too. It can be used to create implements of punishment - the bullwhip, as used for flogging. No doubt it was used in this context in its walking cane form also to emulate its original function in life - but the less said about that, the better. It can also be rendered down to form glue, which is a sticky end, and an awful pun, following a distinguished career fathering herds of cows.

Thankfully, bull baiting is an activity of the past, but man's best friend can still enjoy munching on our poor old retired bull. Following his visit to the abattoir, his poor old todger is often dried and chopped into sections to form Pizzles or Bully Sticks. Rover isn't the only one to enjoy a pizzle meal. Though not yet popular enough to open a chain of Pizzle Express restaurants, there are several recipes for culinary pizzle creations and in some countries it is highly regarded as an aid to virility, or to possibly increase stamina. Even as recently as 2008, the Chinese Olympic Athletes were prescribed extract of bull's penis to enhance their performance. I don't think it has yet reached the banned substance lists. There isn't any scientific evidence of course for this, but if you make such claims you will increase the value of anything – and there's always some idiot who will be willing try it. Perhaps Australian high jumpers could benefit from powdered kangaroo testicles or swimmers from a potion created from porpoise penis.

The poor old bull's pizzle also has the misfortune to be placed in the category as a source of material to be regarded as an aphrodisiac. Fortunately, Mr. Bull has too much value to the farming industry to be killed off for his pizzle, but rhino horns, tiger bones and foreskins have succeeded in placing both creatures on the danger of extinction list. It's something of an irony that man's desire to procreate has succeeded in endangering the existence of other species.

Considering the size of mans' brain and his considerable achievements, it's fairly accurate to suggest that this brain is sometimes located in his pizzle

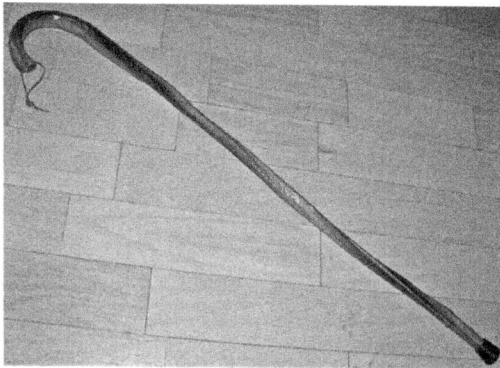

My great grandfather's shaving rooms.

A cut-throat Masterclass.

The old gentleman lay back in the chair. The barber, my grandfather, deftly snipped at his nasal hairs with a pair of slender scissors specifically designed for the task. Every so often he would wipe the moist clippings on a cloth and continued with his nasal cavity topiary.

The next customer was prepared and waiting. His face lathered up and his softened bristles awaited their deft removal by grandfather's razor. Grandfather honed his instrument on a leather strop. Then with the confident strokes of a skilled craftsman you could hear the scraping sound as blade ran across stubbled skin. In a series of quick movements the razor followed the contours of the cheeks and chin, then ran across the exposed, trusting throat. It was almost done, with the clients nose held gently twixt thumb and finger, intricate razor work removed the final offending whiskers from the upper lip.

I looked on from my red leather perch, my six-year-old legs swinging far above the hair-strewn floor. I knew, even at that moment in my young life, that a family tradition of gentleman's hairdressing had reached the end of the line with myself. A tradition founded by my great grandfather and carried on by his son had ended in those vital moments. I was both captivated and terrified, the client still had a nose and both his ears despite the swift movements of grandfather's cut-throat razor

A noble trade, perhaps as old as time, but not for me. Clipping hairs from my own nose is bad enough, not that I knew this was a skill I would have to accomplish at some distant time sixty years hence. In those days my nose was simply the haunt of bogies. The nasal cavity was not my favourite place and certainly, someone else's was not a place I ever planned to visit.

My great grandfather's gentleman's shaving rooms were founded in 1886 on Fishergate in Preston. An old Francis Frith photograph from 1903 shows his barbers pole reaching out across the pavement for an incredible fifteen feet. There is still a barbers shop in that location, possibly the only business on Fishergate to still be plying its trade.

It has always been a mystery to me how it ever came to pass. He was an immigrant from Switzerland. Perhaps northern England in those Victorian days was an industrial

Klondike and had attracted entrepreneurs from around the globe. He was a successful businessman and created scented pomades from his very secret recipes. He even developed his own brand of hair-restorer. A product which, had it been effective, would have been the perfect partner for his main occupation.

Apparently, one of his brothers became a parfumier in Monte Carlo and no doubt shared some of his alchemic potions. His clients were mainly from the town's business fraternity and on the event of his untimely death in his seventies shortly after being knocked down by a horse drawn tram, there was a column devoted to him in the Lancashire Evening Post.

He had also founded a walking club which trod the Pennine Fells long before rambling became a popular pastime, a legacy perhaps from his Swiss background, and one family tradition I am happy to have followed. As a youngster I was familiar with the Bleasdale fells walking with my family having set out from Garstang or Chipping most weekends.

My grandfather began his professional career at the shaving rooms as a lather boy along with his friend Owen. Owen must have viewed the career prospects much the same way as did I, and soon left to seek his fortune in America. He used to write to grandfather quite regularly and I have a publicity photograph he once sent proclaiming, 'Owen McGivney, the world's fastest quick change artist'. He did once appear as an elderly performer on British television back in the days when we had variety shows on TV. I think the audience applause was given more out of sympathy for an act that hadn't stood the test of time. Old Owen would disappear behind a screen and following a quick 'fumble time' he would emerge in another outfit. I think such a music hall act would have died a death at the Glasgow Empire, his screen would possibly have afforded him some protection from the missiles.

Back in his day though it was cutting edge stuff and it had turned out well for the young Owen. His future, like mine, wasn't to be found up hair restricted nasal passages. Perhaps I missed out. Maybe I could have carried on the tradition but as a hair stylist and a favourite with the ladies, not ever having to peer up a single male nostril. That moment in time when I was six years old could have snipped a wonderful career in the bud.

A mountain of guidebooks.

Every Lakeland fell walker who treads the well-worn routes and paths described by the plethora of guidebooks currently available will have their own favourite authors. Amongst my own row of Lakeland guides I also have guides for mountain bikers and even one on the lakes themselves for canoeists. None of them match the detail contained in those by Alfred Wainwright. That being said, the more you look at the body of work by A.W. (as he is affectionately known) there is something distinctly

O.C.D. about it all. For example, in his guidebook on the Northern Fells he devotes some 36 pages to one single fell, Blencathra. His attention to detail coupled with diagrams, illustrations, hand drawn maps and hand written text is simply staggering.

I remember hearing a little anecdote concerning his obsession with detail. He was visiting his publisher in Kendal and was recognized by a couple of farmers who were there on some other business. One of the farmers mischievously said to A.W, "I think I've altered one of your walks." Apparently, this particular walk went through the farmer's land and describing the route A.W. told his readers to turn at a particular green gate. "I've painted the bugger black," quipped the farmer.

Wainwright was quite disparaging about the hoards of walkers on the fell tops, which ironically, he had helped to create via his books. He always claimed to have written them for himself, to recall his wanderings, for the days when he could no longer manage to walk the fells. His work has inspired many other guidebook writers who base there own books on his routes and couple them with photographs.

Other guides certainly have their place, in fact I have one series of little books which describe the flora and fauna of everything you are likely to encounter on your walks.

Books by authors such as A.H. Griffin, whose newspaper columns attracted many fell walkers to Lakeland are probably more anecdotal than actual guides, but can transport you back to walks you have undertaken, or inspire you to new ones with the feeling that you already know the area.

I also have a few vintage books which give you an insight to a Lakeland long before it was a tourist playground. They tell of wood coppicing for bobbin making, charcoal burning, mining and quarrying. All manner of activities and industries that helped to shape the Lakeland we know today. Any good guidebook can explain these areas on the journeys they take you.

One anthology of Lakeland life, (not really a guide I know) relates an early nineteenth century story about a fellow called John Braithwaite of Borrowdale, who hearing his dog yelping, discovered it was locked in the grip of a golden eagle having foolishly disputed ownership of the eagle's newly killed sheep. Its talons were gripping the dog and its beak was impaled into its throat. The story goes on in graphic detail describing the ferocious scuffle and how the dog was at the point of death when Braithwaite threw his coat over the pair and somehow managing to eventually separate them. He returned home with the live eagle bound up in his coat, under one arm and his ailing dog under the other. As the tale goes, his dog eventually recovered and the eagle spent its remaining days in captivity. Why he kept the eagle is not explained, because back in those days there was a handsome reward of six pence for proof of any eagle dispatched. Tales like these do help paint a picture of an earlier, wilder, Lakeland which you can imagine when on your guided walks.

I have a copy of one of the earliest Lakeland guides, penned by William Wordsworth. He and Wainwright are no doubt the two authors' names everyone associates with Lakeland though Mr. Wordsworth's 'wandering lonely as a cloud' are probably the only few words that many can recite (including myself) from his whole collection of poetic works. His guidebook would have been eagerly read by well-heeled visitors and his literary friends on their visits to Lakeland, long before it became a National Park for the working classes.

He was very lucky with his 'lonely wanderings' as there are very few areas in Lakeland you can find solitude these days. They can be discovered if you search for them. You will hardly see a soul if you walk up Longsleddale, even exploring Eskdale or venturing up behind Carrock Fell. The quiet valley of Longsleddale eventually rises to look over the head of Haweswater, the realm of Lakeland's last golden eagle which itself found solitude following the death of its mate a couple of years ago. Sadly, it too is believed to have recently died, the pair having made Lakeland their home for a few years but failing to breed.

They probably needed a guidebook.

"Dear Sir,"

A Lost Village

Across the road from my father's newspaper shop in
Penwortham was a centuries old tumbledown building held
together by soot. It was windowless and consisted of one
dark room. The blacksmith's forge.

What light there was, appeared to emanate along with my
mesmerized gaze from the doorway and from the glowing
embers of the forge itself, occasionally fanned by hand
operated antique bellows. The whole affair came alive with
the sound of hammer blows beating on a red hot bar and
sparks would shower in all directions.

The smith himself was a smallish man who had the
misfortune of an enormous, golf ball sized, shiny, pink
growth on his forehead, this filled me with dread as the
sparks from his anvil threatened to explode it. Post war
changes were upon us and his hammer blows were ringing

out his numbered days. For the moment, farm machinery repairs were still wrought and riveted affairs and there were still just a few working horses to be shod.

Today's farriers offer a specialist, more lucrative service. Their gas fired mobile forges make a good living keeping the steeds of the well heeled, well shod. There has been a recent rebirth of smithy work too but they now create wrought iron décor items. I know of one old forge in Cartmel near Grange-over-Sands, which is now a restaurant with all the blacksmith's paraphernalia as décor items themselves. Quite sad really, but at least they still exist.

These days, I drive past where the blacksmith forge of my youth once stood. Time had eventually caught up with it and the site is now part of a used car showroom. All the local farms, which would have supported it, are now vast housing estates and schools. Next door, the 17th century Fleece Inn has been stripped of all its character, ironically to create a 'character' family pub. The once delightful Bowling Green is now a beer garden and car park.

The village once boasted four tennis clubs, two of them already sold off to developers. Their courts now accommodate more houses than they should. Another is just a piece of spare ground behind the new community centre standing in what used to be the vicarage garden. Its little timber pavilion, which once issued applause and orange juice, has been allowed to rot away. The old church hall, currently under threat of demolition, now houses a 'play group' where working mums can drop off their charges as they rush away to help pay the mortgage.

Directly over the road from my father's shop was an

impressively tall water tower in decorative brick, built in early Victorian times by the local squire. It's now a listed building and did once come up for sale in the days when I couldn't afford it. With my name Waterhouse, I always figured it was my destiny to own it. The current owners have created high level rooms with unequalled views across the county If it ever came on the market again, even though it is a fine building, I doubt whether I would care to next door to a noisy pub car park and beer garden.

The village itself is now officially a 'town' by virtue of its population growth. They even have a mayor. The row of once family owned shops, are now building society offices, accountants and the like, their rear gardens Tarmacked for clients cars.

Penwortham Priory

Mind you, this slow transformation of Penwortham from village to town status began even before I was born. Penwortham Priory was demolished in the 20s to make room for part of the development of houses and a school that I was to enjoy myself as a child. Even its Gate House that once stood at the top of Penwortham Hill was taken down stone by stone to widen the road and rebuilt in Hutton.

No doubt the original residents in Penwortham's now demolished Stricklands Cottages on Liverpool Road voiced their concerns with the same despair at the changes to their village life. Back then, in the 30s, things hadn't changed much for hundreds of years, then within just a couple of decades Penwortham was home to hundreds of families like my own. I've got no right to complain, just by being there I was unwittingly part of its demise myself.

Now I'm sounding like my father who used to recall that the development to the north of Preston had transformed the fields of his youth. Lets just call it progress. We don't need a blacksmith anyway. We need more betting shops, estate agents, nail bars, financial advisors . . . and Penwortham hasn't got a MacDonalds . . . or a KFC - yet.

Bike packing up to High Street.

Bikepacking

I've always loved bikes. On summer evenings I often plod around the country lanes around where I live. I say plod, that is unless I see another bike in front - Then the old competitive instinct seems to kick in automatically. If I chance upon a bike shop I can't resist having a browse. It was on one of these occasions that I spotted the mountain bike I knew was just what I needed.

Having got the mountain bike and installed it at my caravan in the lakes I bought book on mountain biking with suggested Lakeland routes graded in terms of difficulty from 1 (easy) to 5 (difficult). In practice, the grading system should have been given in levels of improbability.

Who writes this stuff? I'm not saying these routes are impossible (well I am really) and I know I was not as fit as I used to be but it would take a cross between Chris Boardman and Chris Bonnington to even attempt some of them.

Don't misunderstand me, my high tech, super, twenty something gear, wall-climbing machine is great fun. In fact I would recommend a mountain bike to anyone. Mountain bike books however, should be taken with a pinch of something not unlike salt in appearance, directly up the nose - then anything up to Grade 5 would just be a trip.

My first real mountain bike venture was over the Walna Scar Road, linking Coniston with the Duddon Valley (Grade 3). I knew the area vaguely from my youth, though memory failed to recall the actual state of the Walna Scar Road, and Grade 3 did nothing to describe it. The word 'road' in this context is something of a misnomer. In fact it's really an ancient packhorse supply route, upgraded in sections for slate quarry vehicles, never a road.

According to my guide there would be ' a few awkward, rocky sections'. Roughly this translates into 'place bike over shoulder and stumble upward or downward as required'. In this case an ascent of about 1000 ft. I had devised a new leisure activity -bike packing.
Reaching the top I enjoyed the view, I had earned it. South lay the whole of Morecambe Bay and beyond westward the Irish Sea with all other directions offering a panorama of Lakeland fells. Now for the easy bit, down hill.

When I use the term 'downhill' I mean 'downfell'. Downfell I discovered is something entirely different. I also discovered that the specialist purveyors of my bright red, chromalloy, super bike, had assembled the brakes with an added feature. A screeching, multi-decibel warning system that could be heard across the fells from Coniston to Langdale at the touch of a brake lever. And negotiating a rock-strewn fell-side was no place to proceed without brakes.

Strangely, it didn't scare the sheep. They just stared quizzically at this strange human juddering past at less than walking pace and obviously in pain. The only way to kill the noise was to take the bike through every pool and stream, wetting the brakes. This does nothing to improve their effectiveness.

Halfway down just as I was trying to impress a family of walkers with my bike skills by hopping the front wheel over a large stone. The quick release device on the wheel gave an impromptu demonstration. Having completed my unicycle display I continued my symphonic descent, eventually reaching the smooth metalled roads of the Duddon Valley.

Knobbly mountain bike tyres are not very efficient on normal road surfaces, they can be quite hard work and though my journey through the valley was a pleasant experience I was quite pleased to reach my midway point at the Wrynose Pass.

It was a warm, sunny day and my exertions had created a thirst that only a bottle of mountain spring water could satisfy. Parking my steed against a large boulder, I sat in the heather and reached into my new lightweight rucksack. My fingers emerged from a hole torn in the bottom corner. A hole by which my water had made an earlier escape. Sitting beside a mountain stream and claiming to be thirsty does sound a little silly I know, but I did drink from one many years ago only to discover, a few minutes later, a dead sheep half submerged upstream. Always look on the bright side I say, I still had my sandwiches.

While I was looking on the bright side, I was also looking down the daunting business side of the Wrynose Pass. I traced its snaking route down as countless travelers have since it was created over 1500 years ago by the Romans. But Roman soldiers didn't have to descend it on an embarrassingly noisy, bright red banshee. It's not the kind of hill you can just stab at the brakes every so often. This is a serious hill that wends its way for a good two miles. As the hill was wending, my bike was whining, like some out of tune emergency vehicle. I think the Wrynose Pass was the geological equivalent of a megaphone, warning on-coming motorists and every fell walker for miles of my presence.

I returned to Coniston via Tilberthwaite and for me this is real mountain bike country. No mountains.   Quiet forest tracks and farm lanes, through fordable streams and along fairly level country roads. All the enjoyable features of rambling, but covering more ground without missing anything. On some sections you can just relax with the wind in your face. It's a bit late now, but perhaps mountain biking should be renamed with a slightly less heroic title such as 'by-way biking' or 'bridal way biking'. Any books on the sport could have a grading system covering 'jolly pleasant' or 'you may have to change gear here once or twice'.

Since writing this little article in Cumbria Magazine some time ago I came across a new little guide entitled, would you believe, 'By-way Biking' - probably written by a fellow bikepacker.

Just as a point of interest. There's an old quarry near Tilberthwaite called Hodge Close. It's got the biggest man made hole you're ever likely to see. It's now a playground for rock climbers and sub aqua divers. This is a hole hewn out of solid slate that you could lose two Albert Halls in. Well worth a visit - just to be amazed.

Some weeks after my mountain bike venture I was walking down the Walna Scar road after an early morning stroll over Coniston Old Man. Whist negotiating a fairly steep section of the 'road' that had taken on the guise of a small waterfall I encountered a group of mountain bikers clad in their fluorescent Sellafield Yellow biker's gear and wearing those tear shaped, aerodynamic helmets, designed for speeds you would never hope to attain on a mountain. On seeing me on the waterfall, they veered off down a grassy cul-de-sac. They must have read the same guide but naturally figured that a waterfall could not be misconstrued as a road. I called out to the leading biker to point out that this was indeed the Walna Scar Road, and thanking me, he led his brightly coloured flock back on the trail, I had a quiet chuckle to myself at what lay ahead for them.

Since then I've done a few trips on my 'now-made-silent' bike. My favourite being along High Street, the remains of a high level Roman road leading from Ambleside to Brougham. Heaven knows where those Romans would have got to if they'd had legions of mountain bikers.

I joined the trail at Hartsop, just off the Kirkstone Pass near Brotherswater and though I had to carry my bike for most of the ascent, the resulting bike ride was unbelievably rewarding. There's not much left of the actual Roman engineering. I believe some of it was actually destroyed by tank manoeuvres during the last war. But a track is suitable for bikers, walkers and riders that goes on for mile after mile and the panoramic views from the roof of Lakeland are just a joy.

I shared that warm sunny day with a handful of walkers, four bikers coming the other way and three jet black wild fell ponies. This, I'm told, is eagle country. I scanned the skies above Riggindale, but I guess they were keeping a low profile. I sat for a while on Load Pot Hill, looking down from my own lofty eerie at the little flecks of white as sailing craft drifted about on Ullswater below. This was a moment to savour and a day I'll always remember.

 I think I slept for a week, I'm getting a bit long in the tooth for bikepacking.

—

"Should have cremated him, he's
going to burn anyway!"

Confessions of an infant fire starter

This, sadly is a true story. It concerns an event that has lived with me for seventy years.   I was six.

Like many children I was fascinated with matches. Now, I could be quite mistaken here. Possibly I am on my own; perhaps potential pyromaniacs all believe that playing with matches is the norm. I can recall pinching matches and sneaking off behind the garage to burn bits of paper. My first attempts at smoking were also around this time utilising a home made pipe. This was created from a section cut from a hollow cowbane or hemlock stem, blocked at one end with clay and pierced with a length of straw. My pipe then filled with my own version of Ogden's Nut Flake in the form of tea leaves – and lit of course with a stolen match. In some ways I was a clever little fellow but this experiment left me feeling so sick it was a lesson learnt very early. Not so my fascination with fire. My little bonfires began to escalate with a search for more combustible materials.

Way back then, we young children in rural areashad a fairly free rein. My territory stretched over the fields and woods for a good mile or more. Paedophilia was not yet a household word, the war was just over and people had worried enough for years. Across the field from my home was Mr Parry's farm, now long gone. His fields taken over to create two new schools, all that remains of his farm are a few stone gateposts standing isolated and gate free, headstones to a lost way of life.

Mr Parry's farm was our playground. Even at that age I

held no fear for his herd of intimidating looking dairy shorthorn cows though I had a bit more respect for his bull. From my vantage point up in his hayloft I once witnessed the bull being coaxed to perform his reason for existence, in the farmyard – long before I understood what this performance really meant, but I was still impressed.

It was a storybook farm, both arable and livestock. There were pigs, horses, dogs, ducks geese and cats. Cats which couldn't keep up the production of kittens fast enough to compete with the mice. Farmer Parry grew corn and wheat, sometimes root crops or sprouts. The hens were everywhere. Battery hens hadn't been invented. They were as free range as we children. We would jump from the barn beams into mountains of hay and wonder through the cowsheds to watch the milking. Farmer Parry would dump all his obsolete milk delivery wagons, tractors and farm machinery in a compound and we would spend hours clambering over them – an adventure playground without a single plastic padded bar or a pit of sterile coloured plastic balls.

It was on this farm that my incendiary interest reached its climax. Mr Parry had another barn to house straw bales. An open affair with supports made from telegraph poles and a curved, galvanised tin roof. The outer bales would protect the inner ones and the tin roof would keep out the rain. No protection from three six-year-old boys with a box of matches. The only occasional guard was a cock turkey that would charge at children with its tail feathers fanned and emitting its high pitched gobbling squawk. The turkey was off duty so we clambered our way up the mountain of bales to the very top. There we lit our fire.

Our little pile of straw was soon ablaze but the fire quickly spread. The flames licked down between two bales and we couldn't put it out. The bales themselves were far too heavy to move and we were soon left with only one alternative – to bale out. Three frightened little souls tumbled and scampered down their straw mountain and made their escape. We ran through the farmyard and off down the lane. As we ran the blue-grey smoke from the blazing barn had cut through the woods and rhododendron bushes to outflank us. I knew I was in deep trouble. I ran on through the smoke and covering a good mile in a time that would have beaten a similarly aged Roger Bannister. Children running the other way shouted – '*Hey Geoff, there's a fire at the farm.*' I heard the clang of the fire engine bell as it raced along the main road to the farm. I made it home, but alas, not home and dry.

I entered the kitchen and my mother took one look at the sorry, black-faced figure before her.
"What have you been up to?" she asked. Mother was a teacher and even at that age I knew that '*nothing*' would not be an adequate response.
"I've been drawing a moustache with a burnt cork." I offered.

I was six. Already a fire starter, and now a liar. Pretty adept at one but but less convincing at the other. She looked across the field and saw a huge plume of smoke filling the sky and emanating from the farm. She walked past me to the phone. I'd been rumbled. Later that afternoon she took me over to the farm and I stood trembling and tearful before Mr Parry, several police officers and the firemen. It was like a re-enactment of the painting, 'When did you last see your your father?' Farmer Parry looked down at me and in a quiet but stern voice he explained the consequence of my flirtation with flame,

"All the straw to feed the animals this winter has been burnt. They will have nothing to eat."

His simple words and the manner in which he uttered them left quite an impression on me. The enormity of my folly had been well and truly explained. No shouting, not even a smack from my mother, who as a teacher was noted for such swift punishment. I had destroyed the animals' food let alone the whole barn, the awful realisation was punishment enough.

I, along with all the kids in the area continued to play for years on Mr Parry's farm and never once did he caution the little chap who had caused him so much trouble and heartache. He was a remarkable man. Recalling the event some years later, my mother said she had been quite impressed with the creativity of my lie and in the speed in which it had been delivered. The fact that I had lied though was not forgotten.

I stopped playing with matches (honest).

"You're the first bishop I've done."

Art speak

By Phyllis Stein – Bit of a rant this little piece.

Although a product of the Art School system in the fifties I never considered myself an artist (probably a view shared by my contemporaries). I became what is now titled a graphic designer and in truth, was and remain, a cartoonist.

I'd always regarded most 'fine art' as a sort of intense, therapeutic affair with a great deal of self importance attached to it. My art school years had given me an appreciation of some of its finer points concerning composition, draughtsmanship, techniques and a variety of the skills employed by its practitioners. I have some of these skills myself but sadly they don't measure up to some of the artworks I admire. Nor do I have the motivation or even desire to create a serious work of art.

Having said that, I did successfully enter some works in the Sunday Times Watercolour Competition – but they were cartoons. I didn't have anything serious to say or the ability to execute my efforts to the same level as some of the watercolour artists I was hanging alongside.

I am though, as are most people, well qualified to comment on the current art scene. But sadly, most people seem to be afraid to do so. There is a huge XXL sized 'Emperor's new clothes' syndrome in today's art world.
Why someone doesn't stand up and declare that the bulk of today's 'conceptual art' is a load of bollocks is mainly due to a fear of being branded a Philistine – or of simply being considered incapable of understanding.

Take Tracy's bed. I know it's an easy target, but sadly it's an example that everyone knows.
Whatever Tracy was trying to say – just wasn't worth saying in the first place. Sometimes when you read the artists justifications for a concept it is just verbal diarrhoea. It is 'art speak'. Tracy, I read, is by presenting 'My Bed' as 'art'- she is 'sharing her intimate space' – and 'revealing that she is as insecure and imperfect as the rest of the world.'

Well, there's a mind-blowing revelation.

The value put on some of these works is another issue. It matters little to me if Tracy herself has made millions, good luck to her. In fact from what I've seen of her I quite like her – but I wouldn't call her an artist.

Next time you visit a gallery read the little blurbs adjacent to the works. It is in the main, simply 'art speak' – a jumble of pseudo intellectual phrases designed to create some kind of mystique. Generally you will find that whatever is being said could be done so in a simple sentence – and having said it, there is no real justification for the piece to actually exist.

I believe the current artworld is full of charlatans, and worse, some of its experts and exponents are

blinded by their own unjustified importance. Often I think, created from a fear of being rumbled.

Many of the exponents of this genre have drifted down the 'conceptual' road due to a basic lack of real talent. They hide behind this world of 'art speak'. Their work is elevated by the system and the term 'art' is granted.

Well, with my views (not to mention age or even inclination) I don't think Id ever be short listed for a Turner Prize – unless, maybe - if I crap on this copy and declare it as my way of being intimate with the engaged viewer via it's candid exploration of universal emotions. All this consummate storytelling and sharing my personal space would be termed confessional art.

I lifted the underlined verbiage of that last bullshit paragraph from some actual 'art speak' concerning Tracy's Bed.

I rest my case.

Off road Alpine boots.

It has always been something of a mystery to me, why my great grandfather emigrated from the beautiful Appenzell region of Switzerland towards the end of the nineteenth century, to eventually settle in Smokey Preston, Lancashire. It does on the surface seem to be a strange move but perhaps the appeal of a northern cotton town was that Victorian industrial Lancashire may have been perceived as the European 'Klondike' and offered opportunities for the enterprising spirit.

Perhaps he was Jewish and had witnessed anti Semitism back in his hometown which was possibly the reason he Anglicized his name from Beaumann to Bomont. Supporting this notion are a few Jacobs we discovered in his family tree. No doubt a simple DNA test could throw light on this if I were really concerned. I'd like to think I was part Jewish but I don't really want some test to tell me I'm not. On the other hand he may just have wanted to assimilate, become very British and changed his name for other than just business purposes.

Certainly, he was successful in that respect. He was a barber by trade and set up his shaving rooms on the main shopping road in the town centre. Old photographs of the town feature his incredibly long barber's pole reaching out across the road. Apart from cutting hair and shaving a client list of leading local business men and professional gentlemen, he created hair restoring remedies and various pomades from his secret recipes. Apparently one of his brothers was a Parfumier in Monte Carlo who must have given him some advice. My mother used to have his pestle and mortar and his ledger book (with its recipes removed) but contained lists of exotic ingredients obtained from companies in London via a legion of commercial travellers who travelled around Britain.

His young English wife with the delightfully English name of Jane Quartermain, died when she was quite young along with her third child Oscar. His first born Theodore, my grandfather, took over the business after being apprenticed to his father. He'd started out as a lather boy along with his friend who soon decided that life had more to offer than brushing soap on to elderly faces and set off to seek his fortune in America. Amongst my grandfather's letters were a number from his friend who had eventually found fame as Owen McGivney, a quick-change artist on the U.S. Vaudeville circuit. He did once appear on British TV as a ninety odd year old still just about strutting his stuff, perhaps not as 'quick-change' as he'd been in his prime and as he'd emerge from his screen each time the applause was offered more out of sympathy.

As a nipper I would watch in awe as my grandfather's cut throat razor would deftly follow the contours of elderly faces and I'd be struck with horror as his long pointed scissors would penetrate nasal cavities to appear again with a harvest of nasal hairs. I knew even then that a this family tradition would end with me.

One family tradition that I did continue was one my great grandfather did bring with him from Switzerland and that was the love of the hills, which may also account for his drift to the north of England. An obituary to him in the Lancashire Evening Post told how he used to 'tramp' as they put it, for twenty to thirty miles even in his seventies over the Pennine fells with the walking club he'd founded. This was an age when rambling was something of a minority activity. Whether or not he took any notice of restricted access to various fells landowners tried to enforce in those days I'll never know. Many like-minded walkers were persecuted and treated quite badly in those days.

This passion became something my parents, uncles, aunties and cousins would follow and we would all venture out regularly into the Bleasdale fells each weekend. When I was old enough to join the Scouts I was already familiar with the local fells and was then given my first introduction to the Lake District. I decided that it was time I acquired a proper pair of walking boots.

Back then, a decent pair of boots was obtained from the local Army surplus store. Commando boots were available but I wanted something more authentic and the only shops to cater for such items were in the Lake District itself. Then I chanced upon a display in Stead & Simpson's the shoe shop. These were real walking / hiking boots designed by an Alpine climber of some repute specifically for the purpose of venturing into the mountains. These I had to have and I had to scramble enough money together over the next couple of weeks to make them my own.

As was the norm in those days, boots were purchased at a size above one's normal shoe size to allow for two pairs of thick oiled wooly socks. But these were a size and a half up and apart from being already heavy boots, they were adorned with an impressive display of triple headed hob nails and the welts displaying a curtain of 'clinkers' – a row of flat plates with a spikey edge to grip rocks and boulders underfoot. These boots were not simply walking boots but real 'off road' monsters, the equivalent of four-wheel drive footwear. They were not just large boots they were huge, and very heavy.

Unfortunately, although my inherited genes have given me a love of the hills, I have also inherited a pair of legs from my mother which resemble those of a chicken with my calf muscles tapering down to almost feminine ankles. These are efficient enough, in fact I am quite fleet of foot, but when placed in a size and a half up, oversized boots they must have taken on a rather clown like quality. You can get away with such fashion mistakes when you are young. People probably assumed I'd simply inherited them from a large uncle with a sense of humour. I'm sure it would have been possible for me to lean forwards or backwards at an angle of forty-five degrees. This though, had an added benefit of enabling me to practice the now outlawed art of scree running. My oversized boots had the effect of having a small sled on each foot. Back in the fifties many walkers and climbers would descend the rock strewn scree slopes of small loose stones at speed where a strong pair of boots and a good balance was required. Erosion concerns have rightly put a stop to this practice. These days, footpaths are managed and repaired and the screes are left to restore themselves with the debris falling from weathered rock faces.

Today, once your boots or shoes get worn down you simply throw them away. Just a few decades ago you would have them re-soled and heeled, or in the case of boots like mine, re studded. Mine were ok despite the terrain they crossed. Perhaps I was not heavy enough to wear them down. My father, who wore clogs as a young lad says they used to get them re-ironed with what looked like mini horseshoes. He told me they used to 'side iron' or skate on the edges of their clog irons on the frozen canal. How times have changed.

What became of my wonder boots? For several years I lost interest in fell walking in favour of other activities and they simply disappeared. Perhaps being thrown out with other stuff from the garage or during a move. No doubt if I did have them they would still fit – but I'd be too embarrassed to wear them. And they'd be far too heavy for my ageing legs. Last year I managed the three Yorkshire Peaks but with those boots I would probably still be trudging round. I'm sure my great grandfather 'tramped' round the Three Peaks back in his day. It was certainly on his patch. This was his adopted country but he knew these Northern fells and the Yorkshire dales better than the locals.

—

First with the news

Bringing you the news from the front line, facing all
manner of danger and obstacles was my job. That is, from
the age of eight when my father took over a local
newspaper shop in the late forties and I was soon
conscripted as a rather small, probably underage paperboy.

Back then, in a pre-television era any news agency was a
sound business proposition. Almost everyone relied on the
newspaper for their in depth news coverage even when the
BBC offered regular radio news bulletins.

It was quite common for folk to have two newspapers
delivered daily - one in the morning and another local
evening paper. There was even a special 'football' edition
on Saturdays. On Sunday mornings some even had two
papers delivered. Perhaps the News of the World for their
weekly doses of sex and scandal plus another for the actual
news.

These days of course, newspapers are a casual purchase

available almost anywhere from supermarkets to the garden centres. The days of huge daily news rounds are almost gone when we morning lads were out at the break dawn, regardless of the weather and when the slumbering population had yet to start their day. Often in darkness we would we would be nipping round the streets or making our way from garden to garden, cutting through back entries and gaps in hedges.

Luckily, in those early hours, dogs were not out in the gardens, unless kept in a kennel. Dogs were usually kept indoors. It was the norm to put the cat out at night where they would supplement their diet of scraps and boiled fish heads with mice, unlike today's pampered felines who exist on sachets of exotic flavoured gunge. A friend's cat hardly puts a paw outdoors and is even afraid of mice. The nation's cats are going to the dogs – and the nation's dogs are already there, having been inbred for years.

The dogs as ever, did fulfill a role as barking alarm systems and patrolled the house, ever alert to the slightest sound, bounding towards the door at the sound of the newspaper lad or the postman. It seems that dogs are programmed to fetch the newspaper, or anything that comes through the letterbox even including unwary fingers, jumping up to snatch whatever is presented, for delivery to its master.

This presented me with the opportunity to get my revenge on any dog that caused problems by trying to take my fingers or at evening deliveries when they were at large in their gardens. Some would snap, bark or even try to bite anyone who entered their territory. I would roll up the paper tightly and as it jumped up to snatch the paper I would whack the other end and it would receive a sharp clout to the nose. Alternatively, I would hang on to the paper and let the dog tear at it before I let go. I figured that Fido would get the blame for a shredded paper, and justice was served.

Delivery to local farms were particularly fraught with danger. Although working farm dogs can be fairly aggressive, snappy creatures, as working dogs they do tend to be kennelled, often on long chains and the mantle of guard officer is taken up by others on the farm. For a small boy armed only with a rolled up newspaper and restricted by a heavy bag which curtailed ability to run, and faced with an angry goose with outstretched wings, its head lowered to the ground, hissing as it scuttled across the farmyard is good cause for panic. Though I don't ever recall any lad getting badly pecked but it was enough to record a retreat and an aborted delivery.

A manic cock turkey posed an even more alarming experience. Its high pitched 'gobbling' squawk and a full tail feather display as it raced across the farmyard was more than enough to deter a small boy. I'd have to scan the farmyard to make sure the territorial minded turkey was otherwise occupied, then sneak to the farmhouse door, post the paper – and make good my escape. One farm had an Alsatian dog on duty which never barked or even got up. Its eyes just followed you as you went nervously about your business. They do say that dogs can detect fear, and both you and the Alsatian knew this to be true.

Those heavy bags were not just full of newspapers. Nearly every home also had a magazine delivered weekly or monthly. This would increase their weight dramatically. My father's news agency business grew substantially within a few short years covering a considerable area. Every week there was a stack of Radio Times that stood from floor to ceiling. On certain days of the week these, along other towering columns of Woman or Woman's Own, the two most popular magazines of the day, the postbag would become two unwieldy bags, doubling their normal weight.

To overcome this problem I would employ my trusty homemade, pram wheeled trolley, or, if I could get my hands on it, the shop's sturdy bike. This was a heavy butcher's style bike, with a strong-framed carrier at the front. Fully laden and in the hands of a small boy this was a lethal weapon with no gatepost or privet hedge safe. Looking back, and now as a homeowner, I would not have been pleased if my lovingly clipped privet hedge had become a regular pit stop for a heavily laden bike,

Sometimes we paper boys, who braved the weather to bring you the news, would struggle round in torrential rain and occasionally we'd get blamed for the state of a rain soaked paper that eventually made its soggy way to someone's breakfast table. Most people understood the perils we faced but there were others, just a handful, who would complain to the newsagent. Granted, no one wants a soggy paper, but as I recall, my father didn't even charge for delivery. Being something of a diplomat, he would inform them that the boy responsible would be admonished and offer them a refund. The complaint would eventually make its way down to the unfortunate paperboy with a knowing smile. He knew that trying to keep a bag full of newspapers dry in a downpour was no easy task.
No doubt each lad would have his own way of retaliating to the complaining customer. Perhaps their gate would be left

open if the dog was in the garden or the paper left half out of the letterbox in the rain. I certainly wouldn't blame them. I had my own way to deal with unreasonable folk. Rolling up their paper tightly, I would fire it through the letterbox with a swipe down the hall trying dislodge something off the hall table or aim to lose it under a cupboard. This was never with much success I must add, but the attempt was somehow satisfying.

Newspaper lads and girls still exist but mainly for delivering flyers which have no particular deadline. You won't see them at 5.30 a.m. or out in the rain and snow.
Back then we were the last link in a long chain. From the correspondent in some far-flung war zone or where a news story was unfolding. Direct to Fleet Street and then around the country by rail and van. Eventually, and all within hours, to small boys with large bags – we were first with the news.

Well, first after Fido.

"It may only be half pit bull, but it still
contavenes the dangerous dogs act!"

My little piece of Lakeland.

I once bought a little larch tree in a pot from a garden centre, it was only a couple of feet or so tall so I was able to carry it home upright in the back of the car. It didn't take long for me to realize why such varieties of conifer are favoured by the forestry people in the Lake District. After about fifteen years it was almost as tall as the house, its roots were lifting flags and I was having to trim its lower branches away from the conservatory. It was a very pretty tree, but sadly it had to go and I spent a whole weekend playing lumberjack as I took it down in sections making sure I didn't have the whole thing demolishing the conservatory.

Near our caravan in the Lakes there is a whole plantation of such conifers at Simpson Ground near Newby Bridge. There is quite a lobby of opinion against such plantations due to their lack of species variety and I'm certainly not going to dispute their arguments. I just happen to like conifer forests and enjoy their quiet, needle covered tracks which are ideal for sheltered walks and mountain bike rides.

It's true that they support less varieties of wild life and plants but I've come across red and roe deer, red squirrels, badgers, foxes, rabbits and snakes on my walks and rides. Anyway, the forestry folk have taken note of these concerns and current plantations are more diverse, so in a few years everyone will be happy. Well, possibly.

Actually, apart from the woodland diversity issue, one of the other arguments against forestry activities, is that they are not a natural feature of the Lake District – but it's not really in a natural state anyway. Lakeland has always been something of an industrial region with quarrying, mining, charcoal burning, iron smelting, gunpowder making and creating giant reservoirs for places like Manchester.

Forestry is just another industry, in fact coppice woods up till very recent times supported over sixty local bobbin making factories supplying the Lancashire cotton mills. That alone is no mere cottage industry. Even the fells are not in a natural state having been manicured by sheep to resemble a giant parkland. Take away the sheep and within a few decades the landscape would change dramatically.

There are still a few original 'wildwood' areas, as they are known, remaining in Lakeland, which is how the area was for thousands of years up till just after Roman times. These will give you an idea of what the 'natural state' of Lakeland was really like. One of these is not far from the Simpson Ground plantation at Roudsea Nature Reserve near Haverthwaite.

When I checked my old boy scout o/s map from the 50s, Simpson Ground's plantation and its little reservoir didn't even exist. The whole place had been created within my own lifetime, so forests can come and go quite quickly. Part of Simpson plantation went very quickly the other year when we had some strong gales. Conifer roots are not very deep and the trees tend to protect each other. The winds took out two or three trees at the Western edge of the forest and it opened the door to absolute devastation. Several acres of mature conifers were simply uprooted and laid flat like the pictures you see following a volcanic eruption.

Later, I tried walking through the forest in a straight line rather than via the trails. I know Simpson Ground quite well so there was no chance of getting lost but it was still quite a challenge. The wind had left hundreds of trees laid horizontally in front of me. Trunks up to two feet thick and lying up to three deep in places. I had to climb and squeeze my way through for a couple of hundred yards like an ant in a haystack before I emerged to make my way down to the reservoir.

The disused reservoir is a tranquil place, ideal for a picnic. The dam was built in the 50s and it's now just home to a variety of water birds. There are a couple of natural stone jetties jutting out with outcrops of heathers and bilberry plants to sit amongst, away from the world. Hardly anyone visits apart from the odd ramblers making their way to the little church of St Anthony's in the next valley.

A few years ago, a patch of land came up for sale alongside Simpson Ground and I casually suggested to my wife that we buy it (well, you get nothing from investments these days). "What on earth for?" she asked. I thought about it for a few moments, then replied, "I would simply sit there and survey my own little piece of Lakeland."

It never happened of course.

—

Multiflix.

Recently I had to suffer a visit to the local cinema – or multiplex as they call them these days. If you haven't been to the cinema yourself recently, you're luckier than you think.

The entrance foyer is a giant popcorn market, a Coke and confectionery gauntlet you have to pass through. And popcorn doesn't come in dinky Butterkist packs of old - but giant buckets of the stuff, as big as horses' nosebags. It won't be long before someone cottons on to this nosebag idea and attaches a plastic head brace to the bucket. Coke is dispensed in what appears to be half gallon paper cups. These are obviously designed to quench the thirst induced by the popcorn. Confectionery takes the form of an elaborate 'Pick-and Mix' counter allowing hundreds of grubby little fingers to dig and delve. The brighter coloured delicacies weighing more than the plain ones, naturally – as the selected bag full is charged for by weight.

When my youngest daughter takes her kids along to the cinema, she needs a rucksack. She's not alone in this corn-fest. Today's film going families can chomp their way through a whole field of maize and drain a Coke reservoir. Her children take on board enough calories to work the projector. It's not just a visit to the pictures – it's a picnic in the dark.

I don't want you to think I'm hankering after the cinema of yesteryear. Things weren't so hot then either. To see the latest film you had to queue round the block, even in the rain, and shuffle along to the command of some chap dressed and puffed up like a four star General – the commissionaire. There was at least some attempt to make your visit an event. They did offer some semblance of a programme, with an A and a B picture, often with a newsreel and a cartoon. The whole package presented like a menu, building up to the big picture. There was an intermission between the films, during which the usherettes would swap their torches for trays of ice creams and lollies, just tiny tubs of ice cream, not huge plastic cartons that could feed a family of four for a week. I even recall one cinema that offered cups of tea, with saucers, handed to you along the row.

The Odeon in Blackpool used to have an organist who rose up from the depths of the orchestra pit, swaying to the music as his illuminated green organ droned out show tunes during the intermission. It wasn't until I once had the misfortune to sit on the front row of the stalls, that I discovered the organist was a dummy – his brown suit festooned with an assortment of sticky missiles, thrown there over the years by non-appreciative kids.

Cinemas weren't all state of the art Odeons though. There were some pretty dingy affairs not quite living up to their grandiose titles. Every town had its Tivoli, Lido, Savoy and Ritz. The term 'flea-pit' in some cases, not being without some foundation. At one cinema the usherette would walk up and down the aisle spraying the audience. God knows what she was spraying us with – was it flea killer, or even nit spray?

I used to hold my breath for about two minutes, waiting for the invading vapour to disperse. Perhaps it <u>was</u> nit spray. And maybe it did the trick. When I was a boy at school, we always had a visit from the 'nit-nurse' but I don't recall her ever finding any. My grandchildren are forever coming home with them. Could it be that the answer to the current nit epidemic is by weekly fumigation at the multiplex?

Today's multiplexes usually have eight or ten mini cinemas under the one, superstore style roof. Each has a sound system designed for the acute hard of hearing – and anyone who isn't, will soon become so. It's an audio onslaught, which is cleverly designed to be just one decibel short of inducing concussion. A sound system creating vibrations to revitalise your popcorn skip, and keep the fizz levels high in your Coke.

Today's cinemas are at least smoke free. There are still annoying coughs, probably from the smokers suffering from nicotine withdrawal. Perhaps that's why they're all chomping popcorn instead. Nowadays you don't return home from the cinema with a hole burnt in your sleeve by a careless smoker.

Thankfully, at the multiplex you don't have that ludicrous standing ritual at the end of the film for the National

Anthem. As soon as the credits rolled it used to be a trigger for a mini stampede to reach the exits before the strains of the 'God save the . . . ' arrested you in your tracks. If you were close enough to the exit you could feign standing to attention, yet inch your way backwards to the door. No such tedious delays with the multiplex. The economics of a quick turnaround are vital. A cleaning team stand ready to swing into action and remove the sea of discarded packaging and popcorn overflow, ready for the next screening.

However, if you do decide to visit a multiplex, despite my warning, you'd better take your credit card. You probably won't have enough cash with you, especially if you're treating your family. But whatever you do, don't visit a multiplex in the school holidays. It's nothing less than pandemonium. Apart from all the noise and chatter, the seats are going up and down like castanets with a constant parade of kids going back and forth down the aisles to the toilets.

I still prefer to watch a film at home, even the latest films make it on your TV within a few weeks. A visit to the cinema is not the treat it used to be. My daughter says I'm a grumpy old man. At least I think that's what she said – my hearing is not what it was since my visit to the multiplex.

—

Going down market

With a view to eventually selling the house we thought we'd
tidy it up a bit. We don't need a House Doctor to tell us
we've surrounded ourselves with clutter and I don't think
we're alone in having more stuff around the place than we
need or in some cases, even care for, any more. The garage
has been the over-spill area for years and even has items,
that we consider may be needed one day, actually touching
the roofing felt. We were ideal candidates for the car boot
experience.

Without trying to sound too pompous, we're not car boot
people. I realize, everyone must say this - it's a sort of snob
thing isn't it. But the car boot idea seemed to provide the
answer and friends have always said they actually made a
few bob when they'd tried it. You can only take so much to
the charity shops.

So, a car boot it was to be, and as with any well-organized
campaign we needed a reconnaissance trip. They hold a big
one in a field about a mile from where we live and we often
drive past gazing snootily at the bouncy castles, fish and
chip vans and queues for the portaloos. The next Saturday
found our car joining the queue to enter the car boot world.

There were about a hundred stalls varying from the chap
who had emptied his garage of junk to the would-be market
trader who had visited the local 'bargain buy' wholesaler
and invested in a stall full of cut-price garbage. One of the
most popular areas of bad investment appears to be mobile
phone covers or cosmetics, which can't fare too well under
a baking sun all day. A wired for sound mobile butcher

droned on and on at full volume probably shifting more meat than Smithfield's in a single morning. A mobile coffee stall was making a mint.

It seems to be obligatory practice at car boots, whatever the quality of your merchandise, to stack it on a hired wallpaper pasting table, with the heaviest items in the centre to test it's load bearing capacity to the limit. There are row upon row or these creaking hardboard displays with the displayed items leaning precariously towards the centre. On the ground at the front, vast amounts of more junk are heaped in cardboard boxes. This is a kind of rummage option for the items which never made it on to the display table. It's hard to imagine how, or even why, some of the assembled items were ever manufactured in the first place. Tooling up or creating a mould can run into thousands of pounds. You'd think manufacturers would be more discerning. If kitsch is your thing - then the car boot is your playground.

We trudged along the displays, our eyes scanning every item in the almost forlorn hope that they would alight on something acceptable. A seemingly pointless task - but here's the rub. Amidst all this plethora of tat, little gems are there to be found. My wife has a particular liking for Dartington glass and we discovered several items, still in their original packaging, and at ridiculously low prices. On another visit . . . er, reconnaissance trip, we found a row of 1930s storage jars in perfect condition. In 'collectable' speak, these come under the term 'kitchenalia' and some of these items are a nostalgia trip in themselves. Car boots can be entertaining.   There, I've said it.

We eventually gathered together many of our unwanted

items, bought a roll of stick on price labels and drastically overloaded the car. To fill an estate car to the extent that even some small items were to be left behind is quite a feat of packing. My own display table was created from the two sides of an old wardrobe which had been relegated to the garage some years ago and had become Hotel Splendide for spiders. This was lashed on to the roof rack along with some homemade trestles. A good lesson for car booters here. Don't pack your table in first.

We'd selected a car boot venue some miles away as it was located in a cattle auction market and offered indoor facilities as an option in bad weather. Joining the early morning queue of stallholders I cringed as a Tannoy announcer welcomed us to 'car boot heaven'. Eventually we were allocated our pitch in one of the huge buildings. We were facing a rather suspect hamburger trailer which emitted very un-hamburger like odours but still managed to do a brisk trade. This also worked to our advantage as we had a constant traffic flow.

The un-hamburger odours were no match for the odours lingering in the adjoining building. On weekdays this was a livestock pen area normally occupied by nervous animals which do what nervous animals do. Their subsequent droppings had been hosed away for the weekend stallholders' benefit but the evidence lingered on.

Our next-door neighbours were a pleasant young couple who were displaying a superior level of merchandise to our own. They were trying to build up a trade in 'collectables' - as opposed to our 'throwoutables'. They immediately purchased a velvet curtain from us to spread across their display table.   Our first sale.

Another neighbour created an incredible display of antique (ish) collectables which turned out to be uncollectables as I never saw anything actually being sold. He was obviously a regular but hadn't yet grasped the idea of selling. Just behind us some chap filled his allotted floor area with a mosaic of videos. No facility here for 'under-the -counter items. Perhaps those were in his actual car boot.

With my lungs having received a fine coating of hamburger grease I decided to get a breath of fresh air and inspect my fellow traders at the junkfest. Were they all doing as well as we were? Even our young neighbours commented on the level of trade we were doing. The fact is, our items were cheap - and that was the key to success. Everyone loves a bargain - even if you don't really want the item. Where else could you buy a barometer for a £1 or a pair of walking boots with just ten miles on the clock for the same amount? A circular display table with a fabric cover I sold to a lady for just £2. "It folds flat," I informed her and offered to dismantle it whilst she viewed the other stalls. After she had wandered off I took a mallet to it as it was a bit tight and promptly split the thing down the middle. On her return I pointed out my folly and offered her a refund. We settled on a £1 and I delivered it to her car. Service is everything in the retail trade.

Costume jewellery jumbled in a box at twenty to fifty pence, depending on size, is a real winner with everyone searching for that elusive Faberge item. Who knows, I may have sold one - but I don't think so. Mousetraps, tennis balls, scales (without weights), bowls, badges, books, everything at knock down prices. We didn't actually knock down the price of one 25p book on King George the sixth, when the customer asked for a discount because they were 'old' photographs!

As the day wore on our prices fell. Cheap items became even cheaper. I even gave one item away because I didn't want to see it again. By about half past three, stallholders were beginning to pack things away. Everything left was re-wrapped in newspaper and packed again in cardboard boxes. This was all a bit too tedious for me. Besides, I'd previously declared that anything left was bound for the skip or the charity shop. The latter being the eventual home for a stack of National Geographics that I thought would sell well at 50p for 5.

Just outside the building the organizers had knowingly situated an incinerator for really, really useless stock. My own contribution to the ever growing heap was an incombustible rusty bike rack and an aluminium garden seat I'd broken earlier in the day.

On our return my wife informed me we'd made a net profit of over £90 which roughly equates to well over a hundred sales. Despite this, the house still looks cluttered and the garage is still bursting with decades of accumulated rubbish. It's going to mean a further car boot I'm afraid. We'd better do another reconnaissance trip. This could become addictive, but it's not really 'us' you understand.

Note. Since this first car boot outing we have in fact become quite addicted and are regular visitors to car boots and tabletop sales in the pursuit of those illusive treasures.

Klondike-on-Sea

Some years ago I was keen on collecting old bottles, mainly 19th and early 20th century ones. You know the kind of thing, those old pop bottles with marbles in the neck, beer and sauce bottles with decorative embossed logos of long gone products and blue medicine bottles clearly embossed with ridges or dots to indicate poison. Most of these were hand made and had interesting flaws with bubbles in the glass or were slightly bent.

Many had stood the test of time buried in tips. The dustbins in those days were mainly filled with ashes from coal fires along with jars, pots and bottles. Anything combustible went on the fire itself. Every town and village had official and hundreds of unofficial tipping sites now waiting to be discovered by bottle collectors. Locating them on old maps or simply by studying the landscape for clues, judging where anyone would have considered the best area to discard their rubbish. Some farmers would simply throw their rubbish in a convenient pond or use it as landfill.

I chanced upon one of these unofficial sites in the sand dunes between St Annes and Blackpool where Victorian fly-tippers had deposited their rubbish. The wind, ripping through the dunes had exposed an area littered with fragments of Victorian pottery, bits of broken glass and ashes from coal fires, all tell-tale signs.

I returned the following week, armed with a spade and began digging into an adjacent dune. It was quite easy work digging horizontally into a sand dune and it wasn't long before I came across a black seam of ash from coal fires. Anything organic had degenerated years ago and only the ash, pottery and glass remained. All kinds of bottles were revealed. Many of these had a local connection, there were cream jars from the long gone St Annes Creamery and beer bottles from many local towns. I came across several tall, slender castor oil bottles in blue glass. Some of these were quite valuable too for collectors. As they say, 'where there's muck there's brass' (or glass in this case).

A week later I resumed my quest for buried treasure, which resulted in a curious passer-by asking what I was digging for. I suppose a lone figure digging in the dunes would appear strange. I showed him the results of my excavations and the following week I found I had a fellow enthusiast digging close by. The whole enterprise escalated and within a few short weeks the dunes resembled the Klondike with scores of eager bottle hunters staking their claim to a dune and digging into the sand.

Typical variety of vintage bottles.

Before I hear from angry environmentalists, thinking that I'd caused massive damage to the area, I must point out that in the scheme of things we were merely ants. The wind naturally shifts more sand in a week than we could ever manage. The culprits with no regard for the environment were the original fly tippers. Fortunately, the wind had covered up their misdemeanors and also restored our Klondike site too.

I can give you a good example of how well the wind works shifting sand. When I was a member of the Sand Yacht Club on the St Annes beach we thought we'd protect our clubhouse and yacht pen from the ever-encroaching sand by creating some dunes at the front. First we built a low wall from old car tyres (all with advice and consent from the Council) and then allowed the drifting sand to cover them. Within a few weeks we had a row of dunes which we stabilized by planting the indigenous Marram grass. It only took a few years before our barrier of dunes unfortunately grew so tall, we could no longer see the beach from the clubhouse!

Some time later when someone at the club suggested that we reduce the size of our man made dunes - it was then pointed out that it would be contrary to the new dune conservation policy. I doubt that this ruling was in place in my Klondike era. I certainly didn't have any complaints at the time.

Apparently, conservation policy also states that it's illegal to remove sand from the dunes but I'm sure there are plenty of gardens in StAnnes filled with sand from the dunes, which the owners wish the wind would blow back again. I think there must also be other St Annes gardens with illicit dune sand in their cement creations.

If however, you do fancy doing a bit of digging for old bottles and your detective work on old maps, or other evidence indicates the position of an ancient tip, get permission from the landowner before you put spade to soil, and leave the site as you found it to keep everyone happy.

I was lucky in St Annes and had the wind to do that for me.

Quack shot.

Beware the eiders of our marshes.

Defending our coasts and estuaries are the unsung heroes of a forgotten conflict. These dedicated stalwarts scan the skies for airborne invaders who sweep in by the thousand, honking and quacking as they take over vast areas of our green and rather unpleasant marshlands.

Were it not for the lonely, soggy vigil of the wildfowlers we'd be overrun or over-waddled by these northern hordes. Our farmlands are under threat. I'm informed that a single flock of geese can decimate acres of crops at a single sitting and that their numbers must be controlled.

Before you get the idea that I'm about to pen an anti-bloodspots diatribe, I'm not. Neither do I hold any brief for these activities. My role here is as war correspondent and as such I must remain neutral(ish). If I did have to take a stand on the issue it would probably be with our feathered friends. Not alongside or behind them, my stand would be just out of range.

I have a friend; we'll call him MrX (to retain our friendship), who is in the front line. He has a passion for wildfowling. Indeed he is an enthusiast for the' sporting gun" in all its manifestations save big game hunting – though he does go deer stalking, if that counts. His four-wheel drive vehicle sports two stickers side by side, the wildfowlers' Association and the RSPB. This incongruous pairing is the latter attempting to justify the former. The thrust of their case is the use of the word 'cull' in place of 'kill'. No doubt these two organisations both receive royal patronage, and for the same reason.

Be that as it may, I've got no problems with a group of blokes who wish to spend their days on windswept, boggy marshes just to bag a few birds. Good luck to them, especially if they're saving us from being up to our knees in goose poo.
Mr X's knowledge on the subject of wildfowl is comprehensive. He can spot a velvet scoter amongst a flock of common scoters or recognise an approaching flock of pink-footed geese just by their calls. Knowledge is power, know your enemy.

Mr X's gunroom boasts some fine pieces of armoury. Less impressive are the duck heads mounted on plaques. They don't have the same impact as; say a tiger or some other ferocious beast. With such trophies you could visualise some tension-filled scene when a hunter confronted his prey and for a chilling moment their eyes met – one of them was going to die. The poor duck looks as though it has just flown through the wall. It probably still doesn't know it's dead. In this formidable arsenal is Mr X's real passion. His secret weapon. The final solution to the duck problem.   The punt gun.

In my experience not many people have ever heard of this dastardly device and very few have seen one. Years ago they were used by professional wildfowlers on the Broads to supply freshly killed wildfowl for the London hotels. They were also taken up by a more eccentric element of our landed gentry as a 'sporting gun'.

Basically the punt is a shallow draught boat some twenty feet long and camouflaged in a dull grey that are just above the waterline. Mounted on this is the eight or nine foot barrel of an enormous shotgun. This has a bore of about one and a half inches, requiring cartridges like toilet rolls.

The punt is paddled silently to within range of the intended target, say a flock of geese, and the moment the birds rise the gun is fired. I haven't been aboard a punt but I can imagine I would be as terrified as the geese. The recoil is checked by two stout ropes about one inch thick. Should they fail the wildfowler would probably lose his head. The unfortunate geese meanwhile are probably headless. I once read an account of the punt –gunning exploits of some aristocrat who set a record early in the last century by dispatching some two hundred and forty plovers with a single shot. Mr X, I hasten to add, also sees this as unacceptable.

Things would indeed look bleak for Mr Beak were it not for a strong European lobby against the punt gun. It has already been banned in some countries, and even wildfowlers themselves think the practice is a PR disaster – that is, if the public were actually aware of it. Its negative rating is equivalent to that of the land mine. In my capacity as war correspondent I have to consider the punt gun as something the Geneva Convention would frown upon

– fowl play, as it were.

My friend has the same enthusiasm for the punt gun that drives the chaps who maintain traction engines or restore vintage vehicles. I this context I applaud his activities in trying to retain another example of British country life before legislation condemns it to extinction. Perhaps when he retires from the duck wars his craft could form the centrepiece of some museum devoted to rustic pursuits.

His efforts, by the way, don't come cheap. The gun itself is a masterpiece of the gun makers' art. A mutual friend once remarked that it was a lot of money to spend to prove that you are smarter than a duck! But its days are numbered. I think MrX knows this too. In some ways it will be a sad day when he fires its last shot in defence of our shores. The menace from the skies will have to be controlled by a few sporting warriors armed with mere shotguns. Our heroes are outnumbered millions to one, and without 'culling', the problem can only get worse.

We could be well and truly goosed.

The lost British cart industry.

In the early 50s the Motor Show at Earls Court was an exciting annual event that captured the imagination of the nation. Britain had an impressive array of marques Austin, Morris, Humber, Hillman, Jensen, MG, Wolsley, Jaguar. . the names just roll off the tongue and the new models rolled off the production lines to an eagerly awaiting public.

Nostalgia of course will endow these models with 'classic' qualities, when in fact the quality was somewhat lacking and the seeds of the industry's demise in the face of foreign competition, a lack of real development investment and not to mention labour disputes, were already being sown.

To me, as a small boy, this was an eagerly awaited event. 'Britain was Best' was the slogan of the day and these new models would filter down to my own boyhood world by way of collecting cards and Dinky toys. I would pore over the glossy brochures from motor showrooms and tell myself that one day I would learn to drive and own one of these gleaming, chrome clad objects of desire myself.

At the time, my own main mode of transport was my bike. A Dawes, which took me everywhere within a ten-mile radius of my home near Preston and even as far as Southport and Blackpool. Together with my friends we went 'off road' long before the evolution of the mountain bike, even without full suspension and twenty odd gears to assist us. I also had roller skates which were almost permanently attached to my feet. My paper round being completed at high speed by the both these transport aids, but nothing came close to my real pride and joy. My own Motor Show model, my cart.

The cart seems to have died along with the British owned Motor Industry. Generations of boys had made carts and they all followed a simple design format. A plank of wood formed the chassis and two cross members formed the steering arm at the front and a support for the carpeted kneeling area at the rear.

From this formula, a million carts were created around the country. In Blackpool, a 'taxi-rank' of carts assembled outside the town's railway stations to transport holidaymaker's luggage to their boarding houses. My own pocket money was enhanced by the delivery of groceries by cart power.

The carts required one vital commodity, which could not be manufactured from packing crates, bits of carpet, bolts, screws and nails acquired from dad's shed - the wheels. Pram wheels, which unless you had a junior sibling who'd outgrown his pram or pushchair, involved a search which led to the local refuse tip.

This was an adventure of its own which would have

horrified my mother had she known but when it came to playing out we were almost feral.

The local refuse tip was next to the golf course and adjoining the sewage plant. Both areas did not welcome the presence of children but the tip and the sewage plant was not policed with the same vigour as the golf course. This was an adventure playground par excellence. The sewage plant itself boasted vats of raw sewage which were Olympic sized swimming pools for rats whose population was on a Hamlin scale. This was heaven for lads who had air guns. Tomato plants flourished here, grown from seeds which had passed though the human digestive system and germinated in the heaps of dried effluent. Urine was filtered through large round gravel beds and the long arm of rotating feeders were known to all as 'pissers'. I never had the courage to ride the 'pisser' myself, but the challenge was there for the more adventurous (or foolish).

Then there was the tip itself where the bin wagons would deposit their daily haul. In those days the bulk of their waste material was ash from every home's coal fires. Re-cycling was decades away as a concept. Packaging was virtually none existent and plastics being a commodity of the future. Rummaging in the tip was therefore reasonably safe. Apart from the ash it was mainly glass, wood and metal and although metal had a scrap value, old bikes and prams were deemed 'rubbish'. What we required were pram wheels and axles – and these were the prized treasure.

The steering system was fixed to the chassis by a large bolt and the axles fitted by clamps and screws. From this a rope steering system ran to the carpeted kneeling seat which was open at the back to allow the driver to quickly jump aboard once the required speed was achieved. Down hill these craft could achieve quite dangerous speeds. Pedestrians were at constant risk of being mown down by the original boy racers – and the boy racers themselves were at risk of veering off into walls or the road.

Now when I look back fondly, and wonder why the cart no longer 'graces' our pavements, I think I've answered my own question. They were a danger to all – but they were great fun.

The elusive shamrock

This may well be regarded by some as a sorry tale of ignorance – but one I think will be shared by others. If you're Irish, then shame on you if what I'm about to reveal is news to you.

I recently spent a week on the Emerald Isle and figured it would be a nice memento of my visit if I took home a shamrock to plant in my garden. What did I know of the shamrock other than it being a symbol of everything Irish, worn by Irishmen the world over on St Patrick's Day and is considered to be a token of good fortune? I assumed it was generic to the Isle and had evolved there giving it an exclusive mystic charm. What else did I think I knew? Well nothing, other than the fact that its leaf was divided into three similar to the clover.

The shamrock's myths are legendary. It was said to have been picked by St Patrick to explain the doctrine of the trinity. This divine connection has also helped to endow it with vague curative powers. As with many other Christian stories, this was written some 200 years after the subject of the myth had died. Indeed your man Patrick himself never wrote a word about the shamrock. Spin-doctors have been around since the beginning of time – they've even spun accounts of that!

Never the less, the shamrock has evolved as a symbol for all things Irish. It was even worn under threat of death as a symbol of rebellion in the 19th century. against the English. Yet here was one Englishman (though I think did have an Irish granny) who was determined to obtain a specimen.

These days I've no doubt it is illegal to transport wild flora from one country to another – I figured the penalty would be less severe.

I scoured the hedgerows, fields and bogs for my elusive shamrock without success. A travelling companion told me that he had one in his garden and that it bore pink flowers. He offered to provide me with a cutting – but that just wouldn't be Irish. This was May, so my shy shamrock could well be in flower – but alas, it remained hidden. Maybe the little people had conspired to withhold it from me. In desperation I called in at a garden centre. "This may be a stupid question," I began, and asked the couple behind the counter if they could help in my quest. At this point the Irish couple could well have taken the proverbial Mick (if you can do that in Ireland) but they were either very good actors or they suffered the same level of ignorance as myself. "Shamrock, this time of year", said the woman,"I don't think so." The man suggested that perhaps clover would do. They both concluded that it was a wild flower and not the sort of thing they stocked anyway. So much for the professionals, a clover indeed, I could find that in my own garden.

On the return ferry I decided to treat myself to a bar of chocolate from the duty free shop. The first for a week following a Guinness diet. There on the first shelf I saw, was a souvenir of Ireland – a packet of shamrock seeds. My quest was over.

Returning home I went straight to the fount of all information – Google, and typed in the magic word '*shamrock*'. It would have made sense to have done this in the first place but my quest had only begun when I'd first stepped ashore in Ireland. Google's response was a bolt from the green – '*The shamrock is a three leafed white clover*'. I was stunned, I was expecting a wild flower but not actually clover, regarded by many as a weed. Not even a sub species or anything exotic. A simple weed that grows the world over. Perhaps that is the magic of the shamrock – it grows wherever there are Irishmen! The seed purveyors in Dublin really are taking the Mick. 1.95 Euros for a packet of weed seeds that I've also paid in the past to get rid of. How many Irishmen have done the same?

It turns out that the word *shamrock* is just an anglicized version of the Irish *seamrog* for clover. There have been many studies to determine which of the several varieties of **trifolium** is the definitive one and there are quite a few contenders. Even the experts are divided. The botanist Charles Nelson backed **trifolium dubium** (lesser trefoil) as his favourite in the shamrock stakes. It's still just a clover. Nothing more, and as for the shamrock bringing good luck, try telling that to an Irish gardener.

Even the humble **oxalis acetosellar** (wood sorrel) gets a shout in this debate. I think my friend must have a pink flowered variety of **oxalis** in his garden. There are umpteen of these, I've got a dark red leafed one in my conservatory – if that ever gets the final shamrock vote it'll be a big colourful culture shock for the Irish.

The Great Lord Esk

Relaxing in my rocky throne, perched high on the top of
Bowfell, I was, for the moment, the Great Lord Esk, Viking
King of Cumbria. I was busy doing nothing while the
world went about its business. Brilliant. Free time to be
king for the afternoon is one of the perks of being
freelance. The downside is that you don't get paid. Time it
would seem is something you can buy.

Removing my boots, I placed tired feet on the royal
footstool (a rock) and drank from my carved bone goblet
(luke-warm tea from a plastic cup). My kingdom lay before
me. The view from Bowfell, just along from The Crinkle
Crags, really is spectacular. The rocky mass of the Scafells
are your immediate neighbours and you look down on the
Langdale Pikes. Bowfell is the hub from which various
valleys radiate and interrupted views of most of the
Lakeland fells are yours (with my royal consent).

It was a perfect, cloud-free, sunny winter's afternoon and
hardly a breath of wind to chill the air. The bright sun
picked out the golden ribbon of the River Esk meandering
its way down the valley below. The silence was only broken
by the croaking of ravens as they hovered and tumbled
about, waiting for pickings from the royal table (beef paste
sandwiches)

I glanced across at the sun and recalled how a couple of
years previously I had stood on the balcony of a yacht club
in Germany (sand yacht sailing not longboat) watching the
sun setting over the North Sea. As the huge red disc
balanced on the water's edge a German sailing friend,

pointed to his wrist watch and informed me it would take exactly four minutes for the sun to disappear below the horizon. Sure enough, to the second, the last glimpse of the sun was gone.

I mused on this and looked back towards the sun, trying to calculate how many sun diameters were left in my afternoon. It wasn't too high in the sky and my calculations reached about six. Allowing for the fact that my immediate horizon was the Scafell range, I could allow for another two suns. It suddenly dawned on me it would soon be dusk. My afternoon had just 32 minutes to go. I had to get down Bowfell and descend The Band in half an hour.

Though not exactly desperate - after all, the light doesn't switch off the moment the sun goes down - I was aware that Bowfell and The Crinkles form a natural curtain to the end of the Langdale valley and The Band would be in shadow.

Granted, I had set off a bit late in the day for a winter walk, but I was only popping up Bowfell. It had taken me a little longer than expected to scramble up Rosset Gill and I had dragged my feet a bit round Angle Tarn. But the light factor hadn't really occurred to me, it was such a bright, cloudless day.

Boots back on and everything packed away, I picked my way off the rock- strewn summit and within half a sun I was on the path. I got a bit of a move on. Should have set out earlier I thought to myself, I hate rushing. My map showed the path down from the summit would strike off to the right and down to the Three Tarns. There was a bit of snow about and the path was not that clear. Eventually I spotted some loose stones going off to the right and, following them, began my decent.

The path became steep. Very steep. In fact by the time I was half way down it was just fine scree. I realised that I was in one of the Bowfell Links, a series of deep gullies that drop steeply down Bowfell's southern flank. What, I wondered was at the bottom. Did it run into an area of scree, which I could negotiate, or would I be stranded at the top of some precipitous drop? I tuned to look back up. What I had originally figured to look quite steep now looked horrendously vertical and the stones under hand and foot were very loose. I had only about four suns to go on my solar clock too. I decided to go back up rather than risk the unknown perils below.

I'm not very good on heights at the best of time and I slowly and gingerly clawed my way upward on my stomach, not daring to rush. Every stone seemed to be a loose one and I would hear it clattering its way down behind me. What on earth was I doing here? Only a few suns ago I was enjoying the views of my kingdom from my rocky throne. Now I was scrambling on my tum from this geological rubble chute.

Eventually it leveled out and I was able to stand. I looked back down. It seemed absurd that I could have considered this to be a path. It didn't even look like a path. I suppose the fact is I was in a hurry and I wanted it to be one. The actual path was just further on. An unmistakable, highly eroded and highly visible one.

By now my sun clock was almost out of units. I couldn't actually see the sun any more. The sky was still light but the day was gone.

I scrambled down to the Three Tarns and made my way as quickly as I could down The Band. By the time I was half way it had tuned quite dark. Looking back, the hills were just a black silhouette against a darkening sky.

Reaching the final pitch I could see the lights from the farm twinkling far below me, they appeared to be almost directly below. It had been a clear, cloudless day, so even though it was now quite dark, you could see where to put you feet and I was able to pick my way down. I did have a torch but resisted using it in case someone thought it was a signal from a walker in distress.

The Great Lord Esk, Viking King of Cumbria found himself stranded in a farmyard. His trials were not yet over. Following the sounds of someone hammering, he stumbled through the labyrinth of farm buildings to a dimly lit barn. Thor stopped hammering when he saw his King enter requesting the escape route from his maze.

The farmer is probably well used to the strange antics of the public on his land and pointed me in the right direction - along with a well-deserved withering look. I shuffled out and disappeared into the blackness.

Well, I've learnt that winter walks should start early (we both know that already really). And you've learnt that the sun takes four minutes to travel the distance equal to its own diameter.

The Great Lord Esk has abdicated.

To sleep, to dream, perchance to fly.

Like many people I have a rather pleasant recurring dream in which I can fly. I can glide effortlessly through the air above the fields and trees. No doubt some dream analyst will have a name for this phenomena and trot out a reason for it - but I'm not looking for an explanation. If I discover why I have them, I may lose them.

It's all the more remarkable that I should have such dreams because whilst I am awake I suffer from vertigo. If I am out walking in the fells I try to avoid precipitous areas.
High buildings and bridges fill me with dread. As a boy I was an agile tree climber but was wimpishly restricted to the lower branches. Perhaps in some perverse way, the dream is linked to the phobia, but then I don't have

dreams about cute little spiders.

Strange as all this is, you may find it stranger still that I should try the sport of paragliding (a sort of cross between a parachute and a glider). I put it down to a personal challenge. My daughter puts it down to some form of lunacy.
One of us is right.

I got the urge to try it, having come across a group of chaps launching their paragliders from the summit of a Lakeland fell and watched them soaring to and fro prior to floating down to their parked cars a good mile or so away (as the crow flies).

Having sourced a school for this activity I duly attended and was instructed on the basic principals of the whole procedure. Interesting as it all is, I won't spell out all the technical stuff, I could lose you to a recurring dream of your own - but I will describe a paraglider for you.

Basically, the paraglider, or canopy as they refer to them, is in effect a large self inflating 'wing' made from lightweight fabric. Self inflating via an open leading edge and the individual 'cells' forming a large aerofoil section, below which the pilot is suspended on a multitude of very fine lines. These in turn are fixed to a series of strong webbing straps called risers and are attached to the pilot's harness. The lines themselves are the method by which the whole affair is manoeuvred through two simple hand controls. This is achieved by altering the angle of attack of the wing to the wind on either side which enables you to turn, stall or penetrate the oncoming wind and thus 'pilot' yourself.

Obviously there is more to it than this but you should have the basic idea - you there at the back, wake up, I'm going to test you at the end.

Once airborne the pilot really is 'at one' with the wing, because body weight is an integral part of the whole balance of the craft. Actually getting airborne is the skilful bit, flying is relatively easy. 'Ground control' as they call it, is the key to the whole procedure.

The Alpine launch method developed by skiers, involves skiing downhill with the canopy behind you and the inflating wing once overhead will lift you clear of the piste - rather like an oversized kite. In stronger winds the pilot launches by tuning to face the canopy and hoists it upward, turning back quickly as it lifts the pilot into the launch.

Sounds pretty simple doesn't it (just say yes) and in essence it is. In practice it's like anything else., it requires practice. To the average novice it can be a bit of a handful. You are faced with several hundred very fine lines which have a tendency whilst on the ground to self knit and even at the point of launch the canopy can transform itself into a giant tent. This can overshoot the hopeful pilot and dive to one side or the other and then subject its victim to a form of automatic pre packing. Some half hour of untangling later the whole process can be repeated.

As you progress you launch from higher up the hill until your first real flight is achieved and you soar in an accelerated area of wind as it flows up the hill.

Now here's the strange thing. There's no vertigo effect. I think this comes from the fact that you can't actually fall off anything, you already have done. On my first real flight, there I was, a couple of hundred feet above ground, hanging beneath a huge canopy and slowly gliding towards my intended target, a landing field some distance away. Below me was a farmhouse, some trees, stone walls, I was flying, it was real.

Landing is quite simple (and guaranteed). I'm not saying I did it perfectly every time but it's not an area for panic or worry. If done the way you're taught you simply land into wind and there should me no more impact than stepping off a box. Most new pilots end up rolling about like a rabbit in a sack - but they soon get the hang of it. Qualified pilots, male and female and of all ages (including Oldies) can become very skilful and achieve incredible distances and heights via the thermals.

My own venture into dizzy heights was low by comparison but quite high enough for me. Following one of my lessons I was invited to fly with the experts from Pendle Hill in Lancashire - the home of Pendle witches, though I didn't see any in flight. Unfortunately my training canopy had a forward speed about equal to that of the oncoming wind and instead of penetrating the wind I was slowly taken up on the 'lift band' of air. As I glanced down, Pendle Hill was some way below like a giant whale and my instructor had become one of the assembled distant specks.

The wind was buffeting the canopy and I felt a few bumps. Then it began to swing like a pendulum. I was reasonably well trained as to how to reflate a partially collapsed canopy if I was required to do so. However, they are designed to self correct and I was quite happy to let it do its stuff. Looking down was bad enough in the circumstances, I didn't want to look up at the problem either. This could be interpreted as 'freezing' under stress, but I prefer to think of it as fear control - or doom denial.

At this point the distant speck was trying to contact me on the two way radio regarding my failure to manoeuvre. The radio however had decided that this was a good time to malfunction, at least one way. It was also at this point that I radioed my own message. A simple, two word expletive,F***IN 'ELL !, given extra emphasis by the slow drawn vowels of my Lancashire accent. Two words that said it all really, the predicament and raw fear encapsulated in two words.

It has occurred to me since that the same two words must have been uttered as a parting shot to the world by countless victims of impending doom. It's a pity Nelson didn't think to utter them to Hardy. General Custer, Neil Armstrong, Joan of Ark, all could have given respectability to such a wonderful phrase.

I'm not one to panic, though fear can be a difficult emotion to dispel. Self control is the key and I think I did rather well considering my phobia. I let the craft fly backwards out of the lift band and slowly guided it back to earth. Actually it all became quite enjoyable and I landed safely some distance away from the amused specks. My instructor had me re-launch myself straight away. A sort of get back on your horse thing.

Am I still flying? Well, actually no. Not because I didn't enjoy it though, more to do with cost. At the time I was racing sand yachts and couldn't really justify the cost of pursuing two activities. The fact that I kept reading about people damaging themselves badly on paragliders didn't have any bearing on my reluctance to invest (honest).

I'm glad I didn't look up at the time by the way. I was informed later that one side of my canopy had collapsed by about 60%. I would be having a different image in my recurring flight dreams now.

Right, lets see who was paying attention.

What is another name for a paraglider?
What two words would you utter at the point of death?

"Can you call back later, I'm on the bed pan!"

The ayes have it.

Towards the end of the nineteenth century Mr. Frederick Gibson Garton, a grocer from Nottingham created what would become a favourite sauce on Britain's tables. In fact it became a global favourite in time, with slight variations to his recipe to suite local tastes.

In Aston, Birmingham, where Mr. Garton had set up his factory, it was affectionately known as 'Handkerchief 'sauce. This followed on from the rather unsavoury title which was used by the locals who reversed Mr. Garton's name to 'S n o t r a g' sauce. However, his exotically flavoured savory masterpiece was also being served in the Houses of Parliament and was registered in 1895 as HP Sauce with a picture of the Houses of Parliament on the label.

A clever marketing move winning popular appeal, though having a picture of The Palace of Westminster on the label didn't move it up the social scale, unlike Lea & Perrin's Worcester Sauce which claimed their recipe's origins had aristocratic connections. These claims turned out to be a trifle suspect but at the time were accepted as fact. This does gave Lea & Perrins a slight edge in social terms. You can request a bottle of Worcester sauce in any restaurant without embarrassment, but just ask for HP sauce and watch for the sniffy reaction. HP is found in chip shops and cafes everywhere but you won't often find it behind a cocktail bar. I've never heard of anyone asking for a splash of HP in their Bloody Mary.

Some years later there were other connections for HP Sauce with the Houses of Parliament. In an interview by the Times with Mary Wilson, the then Labour Prime Minister's wife, she stated if her husband Harold had one fault it was that he'd drown everything on his plate with HP Sauce. For a time it was referred to as Wilson's gravy. I doubt if Sir Harold MacMillan, the Tory Prime Minister from that era even knew it existed. Questions were once raised in the House at Prime Minister's Questions when a bottle of HP was raised aloft to complain that the current owners, Heinz, were closing down production in the UK with the loss of 150 jobs to be relocated in Holland. A fair point of complaint apart from the job losses when you consider the brand had the Houses of Parliament on its label. Imagine if a French product featuring the Eifel tower on its label were to be re-located in the UK?

With some irony, this production move to Holland came just a few weeks following HP's sponsorship of a big campaign to 'Save the Great British Café'! HP's public relations press release declared that the Great British Café was a National Institution declining under the pressure of coffee shops. To kick-start the campaign HP donated £5,000 and encouraged people to buy a brown armband in support (presumably HP sauce brown). To the cynical amongst us, this would appear to be an attempt to glean public support for the company prior to their announcement regarding the removal of another National Institution to Holland. This whole episode prompted something of a mini 'Saucegate' with a campaign to boycott Heinz products, but the brown wristbands won the day.

Another connection with the Houses of Parliament is by Private Eye, the satirical magazine which heads its column on the political goings on at Westminster covering Parliamentary News as – HP Sauce.

The HP Sauce Company has had various owners over its many decades. In fact the original owner Mr. Garton, although creating a wonderfully successful brand, also created some unmanageable debts and in order to clear these, he sold the brand, the factory and his debts for £150 to a Mr. Edwin Sampson Moore, owner of the Midland's Vinegar Company. No doubt £150 was a fair sum back in 1903 and our Mr. Garton probably retired along with a lifetimes supply of HP Sauce to drown his sorrows - and his meals.

Until Heinz decided to move production in 2006 production of HP Sauce had remained uninterrupted at the Aston factory under various owners, and being bought eventually by Heinz in 2005 for a staggering £440 Million. When I say uninterrupted, that's not quite true as they did have a production blip when the town planners caused a bit of a headache.

Town planners have always had to consider the 'bigger picture'. Their projected route of the A38M dissected the factory which meant cutting the vinegar brewing section off from the main production line. To the planners it was simply another small problem for their Land Procurement Department. From HP's view it was a major problem. You can delay things, make presentations, but once the designer's computer had drawn a nice sweeping line through Aston linking point A to point B and the design passed, the problem was then HP Sauce's. It was resolved in the end by the consent given for HP to construct a gantry across the Motorway carrying a vinegar pipeline. How many drivers on the A38M realize that they were passing under a unique vinegar duct?

These infrastructure dilemmas occur everywhere. Not far from where I had a caravan in the Lakes, special tunnels at great public expense, had to be laid beneath a new by-pass to facilitate the right of way for the local badgers. This was just before it was decided that badgers actually needed culling. A practice I must add that motorists had been doing for decades. No such consideration was given to the Roe deer that had migrated from the nearby woods to the fells and back on a daily basis since long before the old road even existed. Expensive fencing was erected on both sides to stop them in their long established tracks. Badgers must enjoy better representation by the conservation lobbyists.

Anyway, I digress. I personally don't really mind who makes HP Sauce or indeed where they make it. I'm quite partial to a dash of HP on my pasty or sausages. My wife never uses it in her cooking, not that she needs to I'd better add, but I'm informed it can add extra flavour. My daughter always adds a bit of ketchup as her 'secret' ingredient. Were I involved in marketing HP Sauce, I think I would exploit this culinary aspect and feature some well respected TV chef adding a dash of HP to his 'secret' recipes.

HP Sauce itself is quite a recipe, it's full of wonderful ingredients and deserves better than being described in grocery terms under the simple generic group of 'brown' sauces. That being said - £440 Million. For 'Snotrag' Sauce. I bet old Mr. Garton would have enjoyed a portion of that.

"I'd like to book a two centre holiday -
with him in one and me in the other."

The author at speed in a vintage wooden craft.

Mr Sandman

I spent over thirty years racing sand yachts and although I do still keep an elderly model mothballed in a lean-to, a sixteen foot long glass fibre mast, lodged in the car port and a variety of sails festooned from the garage rafters, my competitive racing days are probably over. The term 'probably' has a sad tinge of denial about it.

Sand yachting is a minority sport and I freely admit that one of its initial attractions, apart from the thrill of speed and all that 'messing about with boats' stuff, is that it offered any fairly competent sailor an opportunity to sail at international level against the best in European regattas, or even worldwide. I'm not talking about flag waving or even any kudos associated with being in the British Team, this was a real bonus, allowing us to turn a sand-blinded eye to its many discomforts. I've braved freezing ice-cold wind and water and my body has been buffeted, bounced, bruised, bashed about and actually broken. I've been shaken, stirred and reduced to tears with pain as the blood returned to frozen fingers. I've turned yachts over, careered into the sea, found myself in the dunes and even skidded my yacht through a slick of effluent deposited on the beach by an outgoing tide. I've broken masts and axles, parted company with my wheels and had more punctures over the years than a cluster bomb could manage in a sausage factory. On top of all this – I've been well and truly sand blasted.

It would appear to be a bit silly for a sand yachtsman to be complaining about sand. It is after all an essential ingredient in the sport, part of its very name in fact. A good knowledge of the commodity allows you to negotiate its territory. An experienced sand yachter will be able to chart a course through its traps of soft areas just by recognizing a slight colour change in the surface or negotiate the areas where sand and tide have conspired together to create huge yacht breaking holes. You have to know how sand behaves. Individual grains can sabotage your bearings and collectively it can transform itself from a runway into a bunker. It can arrange itself into a lunar landscape or into hard ripples that can shake the wind from your sails and convert your craft to a giant vibrator. With the wind behind it, sand can strip paint from any surface in hours and destroy machines.

It doesn't even need a windy day to discover that sand will reach the parts that even Heineken doesn't. It gets in your hair, your eyes, up your nose and in your ears and mouth. Sand, I'm afraid is the original self-styled silicon implant – and it cares little where it implants itself. There is a technique for dealing with sand in your eyes by the way. The trick is to let your eyes do the work for you. Anything you try will only make things worse. You simply sleep on the problem and during the night your eye will package the offending sand into neat little sachets that can be flicked out from the corner of your eye with a wet tissue. Alternatively, your eye will package the grains together with a kind of goo, which can be picked of like a string of mini pearls. All a bit yucky I know – but sound advice.

As for sand elsewhere, it just becomes part of you till it decides to leave. You can remove some of it in the shower or the bath but you'll always find some later between your toes or more annoyingly, in your bed. Ears are perfect for sand retention and it mixes quite effectively with wax.

Sand is constantly on the move. Anything, or any person in its path is a potential dune. Its ability to engulf is the stuff of legend. Even the Sphinx was buried for thousands of years. We put this dune-building feature to good use outside our beach clubhouse. In order to create a windbreak we piled some old car tyres in a wall about five foot high and about thirty foot long and left the sand to do its work. Within two years our humble windbreak had become a giant sand dune obscuring our view of the beach. The average motorist who may occasionally park his car on the sea front will know how it can find its way inside the car. Imagine what the intake is for the sand yacht sailors who park their cars by exposed beaches on a regular basis. Sand in your cassette or CD player. Every ledge in you engine compartment, on the dashboard, in the tray – everywhere. My wife always complained that driving in our car was like being in a sand yacht.

Big winds and blowing sand were never my favourite combination even though I did enjoy some notable success in such conditions. I also once experienced real fear. In all my years the worst was sailing in France. The wind was ripping down the beach, raising the loose sand to a height of about two feet from the surface, just above where the sand yacht sailor's head is positioned as he lies in his craft. I didn't have a full-face helmet, which is now the preferred choice, and visibility was restricted to peering from alternate squinting eyes, goggles long since jettisoned as useless.

As I edged my way upwind on a narrow bank in a series of short tacks I was occasionally confronted by the grey shape of a downwind yacht as it emerged from its sandy backdrop and hurtled past. A downwind sand yacht in full flight can easily be doing over sixty mph. I abandoned my race and to this day I don't know how I survived. I stumbled blindly into the clubhouse, coughing up sand declared my defeat. Drowning my sorrows with a sandy beer I wondered just what these other competitors were made of. Sterner stuff than me, that's for sure. Or was it simply age and common sense kicking in with an early warning.

It's not all big winds and blowing sand though. Sailing a sand yacht, or any form of sailing craft in a light breeze on a sunny day is not only pleasant but also very satisfying. Light wind sailing is the real skill factor and the ability to do so creates champions. These are the days that keep you in the sport. I can recall so vividly relaxing on a sunny afternoon following a regatta in France, which involved pleasant, light wind sailing from Calais and along Le Cap Blanc-Nez to Wissant just down the coast. As the incoming tide curtailed our activities we retired to a seaside cafe and consumed buckets full of mussels and more than enough wine as we whiled the afternoon away.

In the interests of cultural exchange, I taught a new generation of German visitors to the region how to create sun hats from knotted hankies in true Blackpool style.

Sand yachting has always been a part of my life and I really do have more fond memories than bad ones. I've enjoyed spectacular success and suffered disappointing failure. I've made so many friends at home and abroad. These days my activities are more garden orientated and I can control any sand I encounter with its archenemy – cement. It now goes where I put it, and there it stays.

Flying high in a smaller class sandyacht.

Sand yachting still resists popular appeal, even when you can now sail one straight from the box so to speak. Perhaps there is more competition for sporting choice these days; it can't be the sand factor. Anyone looking for a new sport wouldn't really be aware of its invasive qualities. One thing is sure. Any newcomer can wear a full-face helmet and a fully sealed suit – but I bet they'll still end up with sand in unmentionable places. It's all part of the game.

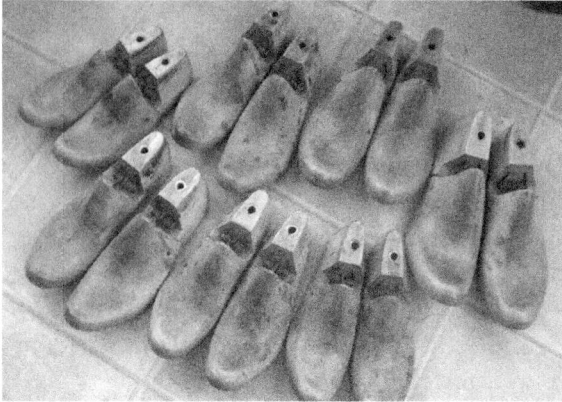

Northern Sole

Some time ago I wrote a little article about our initiation into the world of the car boot and have to admit that we have since become quite knowledgeable regarding the value of various collectables and my wife and I can both spot a bargain amongst the mountainous jumble of tat on display at car boot and table top sales.

We don't really collect anything other than the odd item, which takes our fancy. It's like a game, a challenge, where the object is to make a profit, however small, though the minimum margin stands at about 100%. Our bookshelf displays a host of reference books on antique and vintage items. Knowledge is power as the saying goes, and it never ceases to amaze us that even today with the plethora of TV programmes on the subject, vendors will still part with items of value for a song at car boot and table top sales.

A few weeks ago whilst on this quest at a village tabletop sale, I came across a whole set of cobbler's wooden lasts.

There were seven sets from size 4 to size 10, displayed in a row amidst a range of tools and a cast iron bench mounted cobblers vice. They had been discovered by the stallholder in a retired Lancashire cobbler's workshop. My initial thoughts were that they would make wonderful décor items. All they needed was a bit of a clean up and then used to create bookends or table lamp bases – or, if you pardon the pun, these wooden feet could simply stand on their own. Everything about them was aesthetically pleasing from their wonderfully crafted shape, the delicate grain of the wood and the crafted metal springs, which joined the two adjusting sections of each foot together.

In exchange for just a few pounds, I took enthusiastic possession of seven sets of cobbler's lasts and it was only on my way home as I mused on my purchase, did any doubt regarding a profit cross my mind. Fourteen wooden feet could take some shifting! Not everyone wants a wooden foot, however attractive it may be. I decided, there and then, to try and offload my problem on to eBay and let someone else take on the task of what to do with fourteen wooden feet. My wife simply said that she expected nothing less than for me to at least double my money. It was a challenge that could only be met with success, or my bargain hunting credibility would be in question.

The photograph above illustrates the listing I'd placed on eBay within an hour of returning home - and within another hour I had a request from an interested cobbler for detailed measurement information and also if possible, a side view of a last on my eBay listing. His 'cobbler speak' was all something of a mystery to me but he obviously knew what he was talking about, I had simply to translate this into figures that could be emailed to him - and received an instant reply that he would check against his own collection of lasts and would get back to me.

Unfortunately for my cobbler-talking correspondent, another eBaying cobbler snapped up my feet at a 'Buy-it-now' option price. For those of you not familiar with eBay, this is an option also sometimes available along with the standard auction style listing. I'd trebled my outlay in two hours – challenge met and credibility intact, although on reflection, I think my buyer actually had the better deal.

It transpired that my lasts were in fact a rare set of original clog maker's lasts, from an age when the cotton mills were in full production and clogs were the footwear of choice for thousands of mill workers. Clogs were worn day in day out with perhaps a pair of best boots only on Sunday. My buyer informed me that he'd learned the craft of the clog-maker from an old chap in Wales and that he was setting up a business to satisfy a growing market of Clog dancers and Morris-men (apparently not to be confused). Google will tell you that there are only about ten full time clog makers and an unknown number of part time ones, creating clogs for this growing army of dancers.

Clog dancing was originally formed in the mills with deft footed mill workers tapping out syncopated rhythms to the sound of the looms and this became a competitive event, which is still flourishing. Charlie Chaplin began his show business career as a clog dancer in the music halls. The clog wearing, and probably ale fuelled Morris-men are more concerned with intricate traditional group dancing and their increasing numbers create another growth area for the clog manufacturer.

It pleases me to think that in a small way I'd helped a fellow who was preserving a traditional craft – and it is also something close to my heart. My late father, who was born some hundred years ago, would tell me of the days when he was a lad growing up amidst the rows off terraced mill houses in Preston. Having worn clogs himself, as had all his contemporaries, he told me how they used to 'side-iron' – skating on the frozen canal that ran through the town by using the edge of the horseshoe shaped irons nailed to the wooden soles of their clogs and creating sparks on the cobble stones with the iron on the heel.

He'd reminisce how in the early hours before bird song, the morning shift of mill workers, would create a huge racket as literally thousands of iron shod clogs would clatter their way on mass down the flagged pavements and granite cobbled streets to the local mills. This was an age when the 'knocker- upper' still existed – a chap with a long cane who would tap on the bedroom windows. To be just a few minutes late would cost half a day's pay.

My own childhood was during the forties in a village, a far cry from those cobbled streets, but I still have the tiny pair of clogs I wore myself as a toddler. They measure just 5 1/4" from toe to heel and my father had nailed rubber strips to the wooden sole in place of irons.

The humble clog was worn throughout Britain, from the fish market workers of London to miners and workers in every industry – but the mill workers of Lancashire and Yorkshire were where whole communities of clog wearers were employed. The working class image of the clog had become a symbol of Northern life. As northern as fish and chips, cloth caps and Blackpool Tower.

The mills are silent now, as is the sound of the sound of the clog. Eerily silent too as I can recall, having worked for a few weeks in a design studio based in an old cotton mill. It was situated at the end of a tennis court sized room on the first floor of the mill, long since stripped of its looms for scrap. Each loom's location indicated by an oily rectangle around which generations of clogged feet had danced forming a deep furrow an inch deep in the heavy wooden floor.

Perhaps one day, with the growth of clog dancing the clog will return as a quirky fashion statement with Nike and Reebok branded clogs becoming the new Doc Martins of the student world. Adidas were apparently official jackboot makers to the Third Reich – so clogs could become their new 'power' foot-ware range. The clatter of clogs could resound around the University campuses. The clog needn't be 'Strictly for dancers'!

"Concentrate Albert, any more mistakes
could make us all look silly!"

You could help in this re-birth yourself. A decent pair of clogs can cost you upwards of £150.00, but this quite compatible with any other hand crafted footwear. The thick wooden sole is just as effective an insulation (if not

more so) than any synthetic material and the high-toed, rolling action of the clog is a far more comfortable, ergonomic action for the walker. If you spend any time outdoors, perhaps tending your garden, why not treat yourself to a pair. Maybe in a rich, red leather decorated with bright brass nails and eyelets.

By 'eck, tha'd look reet champion.

"It's quite normal to experience some initial discomfort with new dentures."

Sieg Heil

For some strange reason, my boy scout uniform in the early 50s included a ridiculous khaki felt hat with a brim which defied all attempts to remain rigid and flat. No matter what I tried the result was a wave formation like some Victorian ladies bonnet. Some years later that I realised that the scoutmaster's own hat was created from felt twice as thick, resulting in a pancake flat brim, affording him, or at least his hat, the vague look of one worn by a Canadian Mountie or a US marshal. Our felt scout hats were produced at low cost, probably from reclaimed socks.

I also recall, with some embarrassment, how a fellow scout advised me that to sprinkle sugar on the brim prior to ironing would result in a stiff as card brim. Fortunately there wasn't a gullibility badge or indeed a badge for creating a caramelised sticky iron. Still, this was not as amusing on church parade as the lad whose hamster had chomped its way around his scout hat brim giving it a deckled edge similar to that which you could elect to have on photographic prints from the chemist.

Baden Powell, founder of the Boy Scout movement, was a rather strange fellow indeed, and his book, 'Scouting for boys', was a Freudian double entendre that his predilection for photographing naked young boys would substantiate. He founded the movement on military lines and his aims and aspirations were noble enough. He advocated life being spent in the great outdoors, he even slept outside his bedroom on a balcony in all weathers. Camping and woodcraft were the cornerstone of all our activities. With our boy scout staffs we could measure the height of buildings and trees, create bivouacs and emergency stretchers. Someone must have spent an age trying to find a hundred ways to use a five-foot pole. Our neckerchiefs were also used as emergency slings, head bandages and tourniquets. How many limbs were lost due to a Scout applied tourniquet we'll never know. Scouting however, with all these activities, campfire songs, gang shows and outdoor wide games was great fun and we made lifelong friends.

The military aspects of scouting were very minimal, though we did have an ex army chap as a Scout leader for a time who taught us Morse code and Semaphore. Both these skills are about as useful as two cocoa tins and a length of twine as a communication medium. I did actually learn Morse code, but sitting in the vicar's orchard deciphering a flashing Morse lamp at a speed of about one word a minute has never been of value to me. These days of course, if you ask a child to send a message by using a couple of flags, he'll give you an odd look and take out his mobile phone.

This cosy, genteel life in the boy scouts could have been so much different for us war babies had Mr. Hitler not lost his dastardly plot and the tide of war had gone his way. My generation would have been his instrument for the future of a New Britain; we would have been inaugurated into the Deutches Jungvolk, the ten to fourteen year old brigades preparing us for the Hitler Youth, this was the Hitlerjugend for fourteen to eighteen year olds. A very political movement with weekly indoctrination extolling loyalty and allegiance to the Reich.

'Blood and Honour' would have replaced Baden Powell's 'Be Prepared', though we would have been prepared, literally, for leadership and for some, officer status in the army or even the SS.

It's easy to think that we would have resisted, but any older siblings, friends, parents or uncles would have been removed from influence. They would have been sent to re-education centres or work camps elsewhere, or worse. Our own indoctrination and politicisation would have been relatively easy. Besides, the Jungvolk didn't have to wear floppy felt hats, my badges would have emulated the dashing ones worn by my new SS heroes. Stripping down an automatic rifle would have been far more interesting than learning how to tie a bowline or a sheepshank.

I may make light in this scenario but I am convinced that myself and my friends would have eventually perpetrated, or at least assisted, in violent acts against those who we would have been taught were a danger to society. We would have been part of the new order, a New Britain that was part of the Third Reich.

Mind you, I may well have never made it even to the ranks of the Dutches Jungvolk. My great grandfather, although German speaking, was an immigrant from Switzerland and had any checks been made, my genes may well have proved to be somewhat non-aryan.

History, as it has been said, is written by the winners, Hitler's death camps would still have been unknown and I may have well ended up on one of the trains passing through my hometown en route to a resettlement 'work' camp in Scotland. Good job I'd had my Boy Scout woodcraft training, my swimming and first aid badges. I could have escaped and lived in the highlands surviving on salmon, rabbits and venison. My floppy brimmed hat could have been used for carrying water.

I would have 'Been Prepared'.

"Goodnight Robin."

Pourquoi La Vache Qui Rit, rit?

I'd like to introduce you to a product you probably already know of – but have probably given very little thought. Why should you anyway? It's just another product facing us on the supermarket shelves but this one happens to have a rather odd red cow on the pack and a strange name, The Laughing Cow.

There's an expression in France, where the Red Cow was born, which asks of the product, Pourquoi La Vache Qui Rit, rit? - Why is the Laughing Cow laughing?

Obviously, even the French are perplexed and there is no real answer to this. At least not when the product was put on the market in 1921 when the original illustration of Madame Vache wasn't even laughing. Today though, the answer must surely be because of her astonishing marketing success story and she's probably laughing all the way to the banque.

Today the Red Cow is multi-lingual, you can buy *Llay comby vavy mifaly* in Madagascar or even *Den Skrattande Kon* in Sweden. In Indonesia she's *Sapi Ceria* and in Germany they ask for *Die lachende Kuh*. Incidentally, in WW2 the crew of a German U Boat, U69, adopted *Die lachend Kuh* as its insignia and their sinking of the SS Robin Moor was a factor in the US entering the war. Since then, the Cow has been laughing her way globally.

Dipping into Google I discover that the original cow was designed by the company founder, Leon Bel, having been inspired by a meat wagon livery during WW1. The design we know today has evolved from an update in 1924 by Benjamin Rabier, a French illustrator of some note who figured that a laughing red cow should actually be laughing. I think that the Laughing Cow deserves to stand alongside Michelin's Bibendum, another French classic. They are both timeless images created with skill.

Had this product never existed, and I, in my previous position as an advertising designer, been given a brief to design a pack for a cheese spread, I doubt that a laughing red cow sporting earrings created from packs would have received much support. In all probability I would have been the one with the red face and everyone at the presentation would have been laughing. Yet it does exist and is one of the world's most successful food products.

All that aside, what is really intriguing is why it is marketed in such a complex way. It's one of life's great mysteries to me, how they manage to pack those tiny, soft cheese triangles so perfectly into triangular foil wraps, each with an individual paper label – and then pop them into little, round card containers without causing them to get all squashed.

The mystery and wonder continues as the triangles can be accessed by pulling a little thread which releases the card lid and then the cheese itself can be revealed by tugging a little tab on the foil. Voila, a perfect tiny triangle of soft cheese.

It's a further puzzle to me, seeming to defy all logic relating to costs or benefits, why soft cheese is packed in triangles anyway? Packaging wonders are all around. Take for example that other marvel of perfection – the cellophane cover which is wrapped so irritatingly tight round a CD that not even a finger nail can find an edge. You couldn't achieve this level of impenetrable packing by hand, yet a machine can do it, time after time without a crease or a loose edge. Another similar example of almost impenetrable packaging technology are those film covers on cheese or ham slices. Despite being informed where you should peel them open they are so firmly fixed you often have to resort to using scissors. Then in order to re-seal the pack, the film will never revert to the perfect way the machine had presented it.

I marvel at the technology that can pack commodities such as flour or sugar. Both these have a DNA that is programmed for escape, yet they are packed, dispatched and shelved with hardly a hitch in simple paper bags. Once a bag is purchased however and opened, to be rehoused in its kitchen storage container – it's everywhere, all over your kitchen floor and worktop. With sugar, no matter how careful you have been, the audible crunch of sugar grains underfoot gives the game away. We accept these wonders of packaging technology without a second thought. Packaged food is the norm and even apples now come pre-packed along with shrink wrapped fish and boxed pizzas.

I am possibly more aware because I've been involved with package design and I've marvelled at these wondrous machines first hand performing their intricate, magical actions. Some years ago, I was commissioned to design a series of packs for a snack company and was invited along to the factory to see the packaging process in action. This was to give me an insight as to what was required and to understand the possibilities and limitations for the surface design. The printed design in this case was on a continuous roll which the machine folded and heat-sealed to form a tube. The snack dropped into the tube and once its contents reached the pre set weight, it was sealed and guillotined off at a little marker incorporated into the design detected by the machine and ready for the next pack.

I only explain this at the risk of sending you to sleep, because it is quite mesmerising to watch these examples of mechanical ingenuity. The actual snack itself is less impressive. It is basically an extruded, tasteless maize pulp, which is quite an accurate description. It actually tastes of nothing. No advanced marketing techniques could ever sell you a maize snack without the addition of a flavour. The secret to any maize based snack is in the added chemical flavour powder. This can be created to taste like anything you want. If for example you have a particular penchant for mackerel and cabbage, the chemists will rustle it up for you.

The complex packing machines at this particular factory were let down by their system of adding flavour. A rather Mickey Mouse affair. Unbelievably, their low cost answer was simply, a row of electric cement mixers. All quite clean of course but cement mixers none the less. The cooked maize extrusions were simply tumbled around and a tiny amount of flavoured powder was thrown in.

As you have probably gathered by now, pack design involves a bit more than simply being a marketing tool at the point of purchase. The designer has to understand how it is to be printed amongst other things. Legislation also dictates the inclusion of a host of information, weight, calorie and nutritional values, best before dates, cooking instructions, storage advice, serving suggestions even allergy warnings. I once saw a pack of nuts which included the warning 'This pack may contain nuts'. However, despite all the legislation and control, someone still managed to sneak horsemeat into beef products.

It's enough to make a cow laugh.

"The vet says I worry too much!"

Shiver me shipmates. Hoist the brolly.

In the world of 'messing about with boats' I suppose the kayak is at the bottom of the pecking order, but for a quite small outlay anyone can enjoy exploring our rivers, lakes and estuaries – and from the comfort of a little padded seat. Paddling in the Lake District I come across many fellow kayakers, including couples, who would fall into the category of Senior Citizens. They enjoy their day having picnics on the islands or into normally inaccessible bays. A kayak can be manoeuvered in just a few inches of water where even sailing dinghies can't reach.

I wouldn't claim to be an expert, I certainly haven't (as yet) tried white water paddling or even ventured out to sea. I have though, taught myself (via the experts on You Tube) to become quite a proficient paddler and have on several occasions completed the journey from Newby Bridge at one end of Windermere to Ambleside the other and back on the same day. I think this is a fair effort even for someone younger and can sometimes take longer than one's initial estimate. Once I made my weary way back down the river to Newby Bridge by the light of a half moon. The only sounds coming from my plodding paddle strokes and the splash of a leaping trout in the still, black water. Occasionally I would just make out a bat as it flitted across a charcoal sky into the silhouetted trees on the bank. Now I'm in my seventies I find that the last few miles of paddling on these twenty something mile journeys have to be suffered with the onset of what feels like rigor mortis in the upper arms and shoulders

To help alleviate this alarming creeping death effect, I employed the assistance of an umbrella, as a spinnaker, on the down wind sections of my journeys. Although this does amuse other lake travellers, it works quite well, especially in an open Canadian canoe – but can be a bit of a handful on a kayak resulting in the demise of two perfectly good umbrellas.

The idea of an umbrella as a kayak sail was obviously shared by another enthusiast half a world away in the United States, but he had resolved this umbrella destruction problem with an ingenious device which he developed and marketed. I discovered this on the Internet and also his appointed agent in the UK (you can Google Windpaddle for more info). Basically, this is a simple carbon fibre hoop fixed at two points to the deck, which pops up and unfolds like a little child's tent. Attached to the hoop is a rip-stop nylon, umbrella shaped sail and controlled by a couple of nylon lines. When not in use it simply folds down and lays flat on the kayak deck.

For me, this is simply a labour-saving (or arm saving)

device, although I will admit that it does give you the thrill of down wind sailing with the sound of the bow waves rushing down the sides of your kayak and the clatter of the bow as it bounces over waves. But, having admitted that, I'm not really an advocate of sail powered kayaks or canoes. I know of several people who venture out on the lakes with all manner of attachments on their canoes, designed to transform them into sailing craft. They all end up looking like a Meccano version of something from the Pacific Islands – but with neither the style nor performance of their South Sea inspiration. Mostly they are over engineered, shed made devices that look more like floating jetties. I just think the owners may as well buy a dinghy or perhaps a small catamaran.

Last year, on one of my ventures on Lake Windermere I was returning from Ambleside but the wind had changed direction and I couldn't utilise my little pop-up sail. Faced with a long haul down the lake I settled into my steady plodding rhythm. My current touring kayak is quite long and cuts through the water at quite a pace, handling the wave induced swell with ease.

About a mile or so down the lake I came across a fellow in a beautifully made, traditionally designed wooden kayak that was also trying to make its way upwind, but under sail. He'd fitted a mast to his craft and a rather basic looking sail. His only acknowledgement to any possible instability was a heavy plywood leeboard bolted on to his kayak that could be raised and lowered by a long lever. It was a typical piece of over engineering which I also figured would be about as effective as crossed fingers if the wind caught him from the side. I think he knew this too as he inched forward, not daring to tack.

I chatted to him as I paddled alongside and complimented him on his workmanship, at least on the appearance of the beautifully varnished craft. Being quite aware that nobody likes a 'know-all', I was very tactful when I raised concerns regarding his lack of any form of out-riggers. His reply was quite astonishing. He said he had designed some but hadn't yet got round to making them – and, as it had begun as a calm day he thought he would test launch his new creation.

He'd eventually drifted into the centre of the lake with no real chance of sailing – and no way could he take down his sail from his position in a small cockpit. His only real option would have been to release his sheet rope and let his sail hang freely in the increasing wind, then paddle to the shore. Unfortunately, his mistaken confidence in his leeboard was such, that he figured he could pinch as close to the wind as possible and eventually reach his destination near Bowness. That, I knew, was a tall order – it was more likely that he'd end up drifting back wards.

I'd only travelled on about fifty feet when I heard a shout and a splash behind me and turned to see that the inevitable capsize had occurred. I quickly turned and paddled back. By the time I had reached him he was attempting to right his kayak by climbing onto one side and hoisting his mast and sail from the water. It promptly turned right over and landed on top of him. A few moments later he emerged from under his sail and began the operation again.

I've had enough experience of dinghy sailing to know that his was a hopeless situation. His kayak was only just about floating. Being made of wood it was inherently buoyant and there was a small pocket of air in the bow, but there didn't appear to be any evidence of buoyancy aids on the craft at all. Even if he'd manage to get it upright it was doomed to remain in its new submarine status.

My main concern was for the fellow in the water. We can all make foolish mistakes but cold lake water can soon sap your energy levels and death is a harsh punishment. This chap had compounded his folly by not even wearing any protective clothing. Even a simple neoprene suit can help save your life by affording you extra minutes. Several of his own precious minutes had already been wasted.

I told him to hang on to my kayak and I would tow him to the shore. He took my suggestion – but he also clung on to his submerged craft with his other hand. I began to try and paddle with the dead weight of the sub mariner and his submarine, plus the marine anchor effect of an underwater sail. His only contribution to the effort was to give an occasional kick.

I am an experienced paddler, and despite my age, I would consider myself fairly strong – but this was like paddling through treacle. Digging my paddle deep into the water and using all my strength to pull it back in long slow strokes. Progress appeared non- existent though my sub mariner was confident we were moving. I suppose that from his point of view, his new situation was at least positive. All he had to do was retain his grip. I did suggest that he abandon ship as it were – I would get him ashore then try to rescue his kayak but he chose to hang on. He spluttered that he was afraid that his submerged craft could cause a further accident if it were to be struck by a yacht.

Eventually we made the shore, my own battery levels were running a bit low but we'd made it. It had taken an age – far longer than the fellow should have been in the cold lake water. The effort involved was immense and I think I was nearly as relieved as my shivering shipmate. "I think you've just saved my life," he said, the words slipping from his trembling blue lips.

This was probably true – but not in any heroic sense. At no time was I in any danger, other than a possible heart attack due to the effort. Giving him a cup of hot coffee I got to work bailing out his craft using my sandwich box. His own bailing scoop was now on the lakebed along with various other items he had not secured. Fortunately, his paddle was still tucked away inside his craft and he was able to get himself on his way, the act of paddling soon had his freezing limbs back to their normal temperature setting. I was on my way too and it was only the next morning did I realize that during my exertions I had damaged something in my shoulder which put me out of action for several weeks.

It's like they say – no good deed goes unpunished.

Normal Brazilian electricity supply.

Coaching down to Rio

Any guidebook about Rio da Janeiro will make a brief, embarrassed comment regarding the favelas, the shantytown slums that clamber their way up the surrounding Rio hills like some fungal rash.

Actually, besides the statue of Christ the Redeemer, which dominates the city, it's another wonder of the world how any utility services are distributed through this chaotic, unregulated sub city. At night its lights twinkle up the hillsides like stars and its oversized satellite dishes feed soaps and football into thousands of tiny-stacked dwellings.

This situation, we are told, is a social issue being tackled. What they don't tell you is that this type of building is endemic to vast areas of Rio and beyond its city limits. They are not all slums and 'no go' areas, but unregulated housing appears to be the norm. Some may well actually have a postal address, a local school, perhaps even be on a bus route, but they are owned by a huge proportion of its citizens who clearly demonstrate the disparity between rich and poor. Brazil, despite its emergence as a large world economy and incalculable resources, has a long way to go.

My fleeting visit to this fabulous city was on route to the little seaside town of Arraial do Cabo some fifty miles east where I was to stay and my coach sped through this sea of unregulated housing and a carnival of litter to the countryside beyond. This area has huge deposits of the red clay used for creating terra cotta roof tiles and the large hollow bricks which are the standard supplies for virtually every type of building. Every so often there are roadside displays of terra cotta garden pots and ornaments, probably created by kiln workers to supplement their incomes. Some of these are delightfully kitsch. One had a display of Rio's Christ statue sporting the colours of various football teams. Football in Brazil is a religion.

It is a fairly short but interesting journey past banana plantations and beef ranches where herds of huge cattle created from Indian Brahma stock roam the areas that aren't covered in lush tropical growth. Every roadside building was constructed in the same 'plan free' style with its single-brick thick walls and a terra cotta tiled roof perched on a flimsy wooden frame.
Every little village and small town looks the same and features its own cluster of unregulated piles. When the

occupants require another room, the simply expand in any direction. All this ad-hock building work in Brazil is connected by an electrical system entirely above ground – even in the city. Hundreds of power lines and communication cables are strung from concrete posts down the streets and then each post delivers its charge to the surrounding buildings via even more cables. The whole effect is as though some manic spider has spun a huge web. Each post also supports an array of boxes associated with this supply. In one village I saw that the electricity supply to the market stalls had simply been tapped from the foot of one of these posts. Live wires ran across the pavement. Any passing dog marking its territory would probably blow itself to pieces.

Eventually I reached Arraial. A smallish, rather down market, two story town of some twenty seven thousand inhabitants. Basically a fishing port and holiday centre. The area is formed from a pre-historic volcano and is now the epicentre of Brazil's sub aqua activities. Within walking distance there are numerous stunning beaches with white quartz sand creating an unbelievable pale turquoise sea.

Sheltering under some trees at one end of Arraial's short beach is a little bronze plaque commemorating the fact that this was the very spot where Americo Vespucio first set foot on what is now Brazil. A rather low-key affair I thought, considering that the chap gave his name to both American continents.

The good citizens of Arraial mark this spot by depositing a weekly load of excrement into the sea. This is collected by a covered sewage canal which snakes its smelly way like a oversized colon through the town and is held back by giant gates on the beach waiting for its release, Desecration by defecation as it were. The locals, knowing that for several days, swimming is not recommended and would avoid the area whilst its smelly deposits were dissipated, but the unfortunate holiday makers flock down to frolic in the gentle rolling unsavoury waves.

Americo Vespucio's plaque.

This is no Copacabana beach. The bikini and Speedo clad holiday makers are less affluent. Whole families flock down to the beach, the female members sporting buttock-revealing thongs – which is not a good look on granny.

Fortunately, for those in the know regarding the sewage system, there are a fleet of tourist boats which can take them to numerous unspoilt beaches in the area where they can enjoy a real pooh free tan, the pale can get brown and the brown can get browner. This, by the way is one of Brazil's greatest hopes for a trouble free future. Disparity between rich and poor may well be a problem but racial tension just cannot exist. The Brazilians are obviously a mix of various ethnic groups but you couldn't draw a line anywhere.

Running amok amongst this throng of frying flesh was a whole pack of feral dogs. I counted ten asleep in a disused kiosk at mid-day when the sun is directly above. Oddly, and thankfully, they offer no threat and I'm told that their numbers are mysteriously reduced to zero on the arrival of hungry Philippine sailors to the area. There are other feral dogs and cats in the town. Passing the central walled cemetery one evening I saw about ten feral cats and kittens waiting patiently behind the locked iron gate for some kind soul who obviously left them food and water. They were safe from the dogs here and as they sat I saw the occasional cockroach scurry like clockwork across from one side of the clay path to the other attracting the interest of a kitten. The adult cats had obviously long tired of such amusement and realised that the cockroach offered little in the way of a meal.

The flora and fauna of Brazil are simply wonderful. In fact the green on its flag represents the forests. On my short visit obviously I only saw a tiny fraction of what Brazil could offer. In Rio's botanic gardens the wild life is free to wander down from the hillsides. There's a National Park in the centre of the city. I saw a toucan, monkeys and several large lizards. On my walks around Arraial I watched dozens of small black vultures circling above or scavenging discarded fish on the seashore. Lizards and Geckos are everywhere. My one fear was that of spiders, but I only saw one and that was simply a garden spider. Fortunately I didn't come across a single snake. The flora is simply incredible. At home I have a few cactus plants which occasionally flower. Here they are huge and grow like weeds.

Orchids grow everywhere – even amongst the sand dunes where I'm informed orchids can never grow. I think if you stand still long enough in Brazil an orchid will eventually make you its host. Royal palms can stand well over a hundred feet. Banana plants and coconut palms grow by the roadside.

From my coach I saw fields full of giant termite mounds. The house where I stayed had avocados growing in the garden and oversized butterflies flitted about through giant blossoms. Paradise, maybe – but you also encounter giant black wasps and this is the territory of the mosquito. The mosquito was my constant night time companion despite the intake of vitamin B and the liberal application of something claiming to dissuade them. There is no malaria in this part of Brazil but that didn't stop them from enjoying my company. At night the temperature was over forty degrees but to remove your protective single sheet and lie under the fan was an open invitation for blood letting.

Given the opportunity I would visit Brazil again – but perhaps not to Arraial do Cabo. I would be better prepared too. I'd stay longer in Rio and perhaps travel by air-conditioned coach to its far-flung outposts and stay in air-conditioned hotels.

I'll leave back packing to students.

A 'journey' of giraffes.

Zoos do little for me.

Trooping across the top shelf of my 1960's teak wall unit is a collection of rather kitsch porcelain giraffes. Actually, Google tells me that there are several collective nouns for giraffes, one of them being a journey, so they are possibly journeying across my shelf.

Although truly kitsch items, they do have a rather charming sense of fun about them. Ironically, they were created in darker, sinister times at the height of the cold war period at the Konakova porcelain factory in the former USSR. Against a backdrop of espionage and potential nuclear disaster there was a flourishing trade in decorative objet d'art across our closed borders.

My little giraffes were designed for Western Zoo gift shops and the London Zoo in particular.

The USSR needed the revenue and the West always has an insatiable thirst for inexpensive tat.

I'm doing my little giraffe friends an injustice here. They are certainly not to everyone's taste but they are nicely designed fellows. Each one is a golden yellow, decorated with brightly coloured, hand painted rings in red, green, lilac and yellow. They look out through attractive large pale blue eyes and they sport glossy black topknots. The first one I came across was at a tabletop sale and subsequent finds were discovered at similar venues over a number of years. Unfortunately, other collectors have discovered their charms and to pick one up on ebay will set you back about £25, or over £60 if you come across one in an unusual colourway. Such was the demand for these little giraffes back in the day that the Konakova factory would recruit children from local schools to paint blanks and then offer employment to the most artistic.

I recently visited Chester Zoo with my family. Something of a nostalgia trip as I'd been there before back in the 60s but I found this current visit disappointing. This was partly to do with my expectations. Having been there some fifty years previously I recalled seeing lots of animals amidst the zoo's pleasant gardens. I realize that zoos have moved on since then and the animal's 'space' requirements now take priority. Zoos are also concerned with conservation and breeding programs for endangered species. I appreciate that some species only exist incaptivity the others having become extinct in the wild due to human greed and folly. There's a real irony in the situation that the rhino is facing extinction due to a bizarre theory that their horns are believed to offer a cure for human erectile malfunction. This has led to a decline of one species in order to aid the procreation of another.

The problem with all this new essential environment for the animals, offering lots of space for them to run and hide – is that they do. When I read a sign which indicates which animal is housed in a particular section, it is disappointing if said creature decides to secrete itself in the shrubbery away from the gawping humans. I did begin to wonder if some of them actually existed. I think I saw a black panther some 50 yards away sleeping in the long grass but it could have been a bin bag. A Sumatran tiger was on a raised platform just out of view behind a tree and one lone lion was sleeping behind a large rock. Other animals were frustratingly just as elusive. I could see the elephants and a rhinoceros but for an elephant to play hide and seek is a big ask.

The zoo concept has changed, not just for their conservation work but now they offer a zoo 'experience'. Chester zoo has now created a multi million pound environment for some of its animals in an attempted recreation of the South Sea Islands. From a distance it looks like an exciting prospect You can see the rooflines of exotic Polynesian buildings on a South Sea Island theme – but sadly they turn out to be simply more cafeterias and gift shops. Visitors to the Islands are offered the chance to board a large, rather crude boat which is a clumsy version of a craft resembling the Queen of Tonga's Royal barge. This plods round the Islands offering potential views of the secretive animals hiding themselves amidst bamboo shrubbery.
I declined this opportunity and made my way back to the original zoo. This has elevated wooden walkways enabling the visitor to enjoy overhead non-views of the hidden animals. On one such walkway I came across a discarded nappy. It would appear that some of the inmates have

better toilet habits than their captors.

I've not always had such a septic view of zoos. I've visited several over the years and some offer a more enjoyable experience. Bristol Zoo is very nice but smaller. Blackpool has a more modern zoo and was created some years ago after its predecessor in the Tower was closed down. Actually it was more of a menagerie than a zoo which I recall visiting as a small child. This was housed in a large room beneath the Blackpool Tower itself and contained a number a large animals, a lion, a tiger and a bear as I recall, kept rather cruelly in rather cramped conditions for their whole miserable lives. As a child I never gave the matter much thought but I do recall feeling a bit sorry some years later when I saw the elephants which were part of the Tower Circus in their home below the ring.

I was at the Art School in Blackpool some years later and we art students were always recruited for the Technical College's Shakespeare productions, which were performed in the Tower Circus ring. Authentic theatre in the round as it were. Our penchant for dressing up in tights and feathered hats was evident and we would populate the theatrical street and crowd scenes with enthusiasm. Flouncing across the circus ring we would descend the stairs and make our way past the elephants and up the other side to repeat the spectacle. The elephants were at least taken out each day from their gloomy stalls and across the promenade to frolic in the sea.

Another small zoo I've visited is in the Lake District which concentrates on smaller creatures. This is far more enjoyable. They have leaf cutter ants which are separated from their leaves by a length of suspended rope and you can watch them at close quarters on their hemp motorway going backwards and forwards with their leafy cargo. Visitors can also choose to hold or touch giant lizards and snakes. This is a perfect place for children and the gift shop is not so much in your face as the ones at zoos such as Chester. The current offering on the giraffe theme at Chester is a three-foot long balloon with a cartoon giraffe's face retailing at an astonishing £5. As a friend later remarked, ' they have some neck charging that for a balloon'. Running a zoo is obviously an expensive business but having spent in the region of a hundred pounds on entry for a family of four, I resented running the gauntlet of expensive gift shops and kiosks.

The zoo experience does little for me. People who run zoos could probably make all the funds they require for animal conservation if they sponsored wild life filmmaking. There must be huge amounts to be made from international television rights. In future I will content myself with the superb wildlife programs on television.

Waterhouse

Psychedelia in pastel.

Browsing along the shelves of one of those cut- price bookstores I chanced upon a book plotting the history of Scalextric, the slot car racing toy. The very thought of such a book could well induce sleep in most people (myself included) – but I do have a reason to have a passing interest. My involvement with Scalextric having been purely professional, as an art director on the account for an advertising agency in the late 60s.

For the uninitiated, slot car racing involves scale model cars racing round a plastic track and picking up electricity to power their motors via a slot in the centre. The velocity of the cars themselves is governed by a remote device, which offers the controller speeds from very quick to take off. I always found the whole affair to be rather tedious as the cars would hurtle off the track at the very thought of centrifugal force. Apart from retrieving flying cars, the track itself was split into lengths about a foot long and one would be constantly checking the entire length for the obligatory duff connection. All in all, I can declare myself not an enthusiast; such folk would never call Scalextric a 'toy' anyway.

Scalextric had another equally problematic product called Jump Jockey, which I had acquired following an expensive trip to London for a photo shoot. Initially I just intended to show it my children but I'm not surprised that no one ever asked for it back, it was something of a disaster anyway. Jump Jockey was similar in concept to Scalextric but with little electric cars running inside a box section track and a rod holding a horse and jockey protruded through a slot in the top. The effect was of the horse moving along under its own power, that is, when the numerous connections didn't keep having the same tendency to disconnect. The control device for speed also enabled the rod to rise when the horse and jockey came across a jump barrier. With so many things to go wrong it's not really a surprise that they did. Consequently it joined all those other items you don't ever use – under the bed.

Back in those days advertising and design studios did have an air of 'studio' about them. Brushes, markers, pads, pastels, drawing boards – all the paraphernalia of – well, a studio. These days any design department boasts a battery of Apple Macs and they are silent but for the tapping of keyboards and the sound of printers.

It was in such a 'studio' environment that I had learned to ply my trade. I could draw a little and could throw pastels, gouache and markers around well enough to impress clients with slick storyboards, package design and advertising concepts. As an Art Director / Visualiser (advertising is very fond of grandiose titles) my responsibilities were to

presentation. Scalextric, I was informed, were going to require a new image and my brief was to come up with something new and exciting.

Psychedelia in pastel.

The designs which won the day (and the lucrative business) owed more to the brilliant salesmanship of the Account Executive (another title) than to the designs themselves. They were a series of packs depicting an impressionistic view of slot car racing through a haze of pastel. Movement was created via streaks of colour emanating from the racing cars and trailing in their wake. The sort of effect you get if you leave a camera shutter open. In retrospect, that technique would probably have been more appropriate. Today's studio would have the effect done in minutes via the magic of Photoshop.

The whole creative episode lasted for a couple of frantic pastel scraping weeks which resulted in my world of advertising being seen through a haze of primary coloured pastel dust. It covered my desk, the carpet, ledges, clothes, and hair - everywhere. I never really cared for the medium either. Mistakes are hard to rectify with the stuff, and it's so messy. How successful these colourful packs were I couldn't say. I have a sneaking feeling they were a disaster. Scalextric as a company, changed hands the very next year and the toy trade generally was in recession for a while, though I hardly think it possible that I'd caused such trauma in the trade by pastel power.

Thumbing through my newfound book I discovered an example of my pastel master class. *This*, proclaimed the caption, *was what Scalextric looked like in 1970 – if you were a spaced out hippy!*

I nearly burst out laughing in the shop. I had to buy the book just for that one line of copy and a tiny photograph – the result of my pastel induced trip. On reflection, it was pretty awful, perhaps I did cause problems for the company. Is it too late to apologise?

Ode to a Lancashire Flapjack

Some years ago I wrote a little magazine article admitting that having 'wandered lonely as a cloud oe'r the hills and dales,' I had often returned to my car in Grasmere without having even a thought to call in to pay homage to William Wordsworth whose cottage was just o'er the road. I mused that I was more likely to follow my nose to the source of Sarah Nelson's famous Grasmere Gingerbread. This, I have to admit, is not strictly true. I realize that huge numbers of people are partial to Sarah's Gingerbread but I find it's a bit like chewing thick cardboard and I'd much rather enjoy a simple ginger nut biscuit (or two).

That being said, and as someone with a former career in advertising and marketing, I am more than impressed by the success of this remarkable enterprise. From its tiny shop in the village, hardly bigger than a pantry, Grasmere Gingerbread is exported worldwide. Obviously they benefit from having a prime spot in a tourist area, but they do everything right. Even the counter staff are dressed as Victorian kitchen maids and the simple packaging has that 'home made' appeal.

The Lancashire and Lakeland area has a variety of regional recipes and products which are household names. Cumberland sausages, Eccles, Chorley and Goonargh Cakes, Parkin, Lancashire Cheeses, Cartmel Sticky Toffee Pudding, Kendal Mint Cake, Blackpool Rock and Morecambe Bay Shrimps, even Fleetwood's Fisherman's Friend – and I'm sure you can name lots of others.

These regional recipe ideas offer real opportunities for anyone with entrepreneurial spirit. I'd take up the challenge myself if I wasn't so long in the tooth and I still possessed the enthusiasm required. Take for example the humble flapjack. You could create your own distinct version, perhaps enhanced with your own favorite flavour. How about orange flavoured flapjack or treacle flapjack? Fleetwood Flapjack – I can see it on the shelves already.

Once you've created your recipe you don't even have to produce the final product yourself. Any commercial baker can produce and pack it for you. They have the industry's health and safety standard kitchens anyway.

The biggest hurdle (apart from your investment) is getting your creation listed in the supermarkets, but there are food brokers who can help you in this area. You can even start the ball rolling yourself 'on-line' these days or take your samples round to wholesalers yourself. I know a chap who now owns the biggest sports clothing printing company in the UK. He started some years ago by knocking on Blackpool boarding house doors, offering personalised T shirts which he printed himself on the kitchen table. Of course it helps if you have a unique selling point. My nephew completed the John O'Groats to Lands End bike ride with 150 pieces of flapjack from his local baker as his claimed energy supplement, much the same as mountaineers endorse Kendal Mint Cake. On the other hand you can simply declare your secret recipe is unique because of its flavour.

Some of these regional favourites are no longer cottage industries. I watched a programme on TV when Michael Portillo visited the Eccles Cake factory that was producing their current filled confections on an astonishingly industrial scale. At the other end of the confectionary spectrum, I once designed some packs for a local Lancashire snack company which was so small that their flavour powders were added by tumbling the extruded maize product around in an electric cement mixer (clean of course). I designed some other snack packs for a chap who'd created a snack idea and to everyone's surprise he actually got his product listed by a national supermarket chain. Obviously, I would claim that it was the pack design that did the trick - but it does show it can be done.

All this advice is offered with no expectations of results, but there are opportunities out there. I can imagine lots of Lancashire treats that could grace our supermarket shelves; Bury Butter Biscuits, Chipping Cherry Cheesecake, Appleby Apple Cake, Poulton Pop Corn, Tarleton Tart (I do like alliterations). I'm sure you could cook up lots more concoction ideas that could even put your own village on the map. I will possibly offer my services as pack designer to anyone who takes up this culinary challenge, but I doubt if my Fleetwood Flapjacks will ever make it to the shelves. Pity.

Who comes not hither on our streets
With tasty Fleetwood Flapjack treats;
How sad such enterprise be missed
And ne'er then our taste buds kissed.

Hmm, I think next time I'm in Grasmere I'll call in to Mr.
Wordsworth's Heritage Centre . . . . my Wordsworth
inspired poetic jottings probably lack taste – unlike my
proposed flapjacks.

"I've seen the future!"

"Could you pass me my rescue club please Og."

Postcard fro the GoKart Electric golf trolley series.

Golf Workshop

Taking my golf problems to the garage.

Taking up golf at the age of sixty is not the recommended route to success. Entering my first competition I scored an embarrassing twelve on the first short par four hole. A catalogue of disaster which ping-ponged from bunker to hedge and back again. The muttering of 'take your time' and 'relax' etc - hardly helped, though I know it was all given
in good spirit from an audience of stunned players, knowing they were in for a long game. Needless to say, my handicap, regarded prior to this by some as generous, was very safe for some time but I don't think my fellow players knew the extent of my competitive will.

In the pursuit of success my bedside cupboard became a small library of golf coaching books and I'd study them avidly. The problem was, how to translate described golfing techniques into practice. To create a perfect swing – you really need a perfect body.

Mine has developed a few flaws over the decades and one, which I was actually born with. It's hardly a handicap, but my right leg is slightly longer than my left by about a quarter of an inch. Something of an advantage years ago on the curved running track but doesn't quite fit with a golf stance. I think I also have a back problem in that it doesn't flex the way it should for a regulation swing.

Actually I wasn't particularly aware of my back problem till I tried to emulate a drawn shot following the steps laid down by Gary Player, Jack Nicklaus and others. Closing the clubface of my driver, I addressed the ball with it just in line with my left instep and placed my right foot a few inches back from my normal stance. Then, swinging through on a slight in to out line I made contact with the ball and followed through in a great arc and over my left shoulder. My eyes remained firmly fixed to the spot where my ball had been teed up till my swing was complete and then I raised my eyes to follow its flight.

It went dead straight. No deviation, no draw – just dead straight. I tried this over and over with the ball flying straight and true each time, apart from a few slightly miss cued shots due to imbalance. My failure to create a draw was more than compensated with my newfound 'straight down the fairway' golf shot.

Over the next few weeks I adapted this stance to the rest of my golf game with the resulting same straight ball. I don't mean by this that every shot was straight and true. Balance is compromised by my less than conventional stance and I do scuff the occasional ball, but I hardly ever 'pull' a ball like I used to.

Now, this technique probably only works for me, but the results say one thing. Do what you find is the most comfortable, not necessarily by the book, but do be prepared for looks of incredulity from other players. Not to mention having your oddly placed leg pulled.

I also discovered that my irons were more consistent if I held the club further down the shaft. What I lost in distance I more than made up for in accuracy. With this new info in mind I started sawing about an inch off each iron and adding new grips. By this time I was becoming the butt of some amusing banter on the course. My strange stance was one thing but my workshop antics were becoming notorious. Lots of jokes regarding hacksaws, hammers and glue etc – all given in good spirit as my game was becoming more consistent.

I then turned my workshop attentions to putters. I tried everything to create the perfect putter. There is no such thing of course, what I was looking for was a device that would help impart an accurate pendulum swing. Gary Player writes that when he plays his putt toward the hole he doesn't look up, but listens for it plopping into the hole. For us mere mortals it doesn't quite work like that but I do understand what he was getting at. If you swing through the ball on the line you have prepared, your ball will naturally travel in the direction you have chosen. So, my straight swing and follow through is in order. My devices to achieve this are legendary.

I would turn up ay the club each week with yet another product from my garage. Chin length putters, belly putters, chest putters and putters with all manner of heads and protrusions. Sawn off putters – some perfect for anyone of about four foot tall.

My reputation grew as a golf club tinkerer and the jokes came thick and fast. I hadn't planned on this reaction but I figured it was best to take it all in good spirit. Golf is only a game and I did take the money on more than one Saturday morning which did keep the jokes acceptable and given with a modicum of respect, at least for effort.

I made a club for the club captain following a particularly wet week. Adapting one of my extra long putters, I fixed a folding umbrella into the top. This allowed the player to stand on the green and putt whilst being protected by the brolly – it would then all fold up into the golf bag. I made another putter the following year, which featured a claw hammer putting head. The swing ticket proclaiming it as 'The Fringe Master' with the legend – Hammer home your advantage - nail those long putts.

These all went down quite well and I did create another one following a chance remark made by a player who was having difficulty getting his ball out of some thick rough. "I need a bloody lump hammer to get this bastard out," His seven-pound lump hammer headed golf club was delivered the very next week. If you could handle it, a seven-pound iron would give take you to Tiger Woods distance let alone get you out of the rough.

I was cautioned by the club secretary one evening when I was down at the club to try out my latest putter. A rather strange device with more bends in it than actually required due to rough workmanship and the fact that it had been concocted from the bits of several previous disasters. The whole thing had been spayed black to cover up a host of imperfections. Although my father had been an engineer I don't think I'd inherited those particular genes. I am more at home with resin and a hammer. "Has that club been ratified by the R&A?" he enquired, knowing full well that there wasn't the remotest possibility of such an endorsement and that it had come straight from my personal golfing scrap yard. "You can't use that in a competition you know," he added. He meant well I know, and of course he was quite correct – but I was more elated than deflated. Somebody thinks that I may have actually created a club that would give me an advantage!

That sprayed black putter also caused some amusement in the clubhouse on its first outing. Sneaking past the window on my way to test it out I was spotted by a group of players who were aware of my antics and called me in. One chap took my putter and gave it a practise swing. It was a right-handed affair but he was left-handed. Never the less he had some tables moved back and a pint glass placed on its side across the room. Taking aim he struck the ball and it rolled straight and true across the carpet into the glass. When the laughter had died down I enquired if there would be any advanced orders.

I was quite happy with that club for a few weeks. So much so, I took it along to an outlet that made their own golf clubs. I enquired what the routine was for getting a club ratified, adding that I didn't want to post the monstrosity I was holding off to St Andrews and become the laughing stock of the golf world. The upshot was, that the chap in the shop said he would re-build my club to the same dimensions for £25 and as he was a registered club maker everything would be kosher.

Two weeks later I showed my new putter to the club secretary and everyone was happy. No doubt the fellow in the shop is still laughing and that same club eventually was the one that acquired an umbrella and is possibly hanging over someone's desk as a memento of his captaincy.

Since writing this little piece I understand that shoulder length putters are now in fact illegal.

My golf game has reached a sort of plateau. Like most amateur golfers, consistency is the problem. My handicap is in the low teens and I know it could be even lower, especially if I were to play more often. In my case I know it's just a question of keeping my head down and balance. My next project will have to involve designs for a swivelling corset incorporating a neck collar. Shoes with extra long spikes and possibly some kind of leg brace. I don't think I'll bother.

These days, if anyone's jokes get a bit below the belt I just point up above the bar to the club's premier knockout competition trophy board. The founder's trophy – and there, following a purple patch of good fortune and studious workshop application, is my name in gold capitals listed amongst the club's notables.

Incredible, but true.

Postcard from the GoKart Electric Golf trolley series.

Golf - the fair game

The Royal and Ancient Golf Club of St Andrews publish
The Rules of Golf, familiar to every player of the game.
The book itself is familiar . The actual rules are less so and
during the course of the average game they are discussed,
mulled over, interpreted to suit a given situation and
occasionally flouted. The rule book is seldom really
questioned though, and I think it is regarded by the average
golfer as the 'bible' of golf, designed to keep the game fair.
The book is like the bible itself, owned by many - but
seldom read.

I can give you an example of 'flouting' as witnessed by a
golfing friend who was acting as a crowd marshal at an
Open Tournament. A player of international repute (I'd
give you his name if I had it) had sent a wayward ball into
an unplayable area of long grass. In direct line with its new

impossible position and the green was a tower constructed to carry television cameras - and thus was the subject of a legitimate claim for a free drop. This required the ruling of an official who was duly called. Whilst he waited, the player in question paced up and down in the area where the free drop would take place. By the time his request was sanctioned the long grass was flattened and he enjoyed a near perfect lie.

There must be a million of these unsavoury tales and I suppose when big money is at stake rules are more prone to being used or abused. For the average club golfer playing for a drink or a few quid, the worst I've seen is the replaying of a bad shot because the original 'shanked' attempt hit a temporary fence on its way nowhere. I think this could be described as simply 'stretching' a rule.

Cheating at golf is generally regarded as unacceptable. Players may often break a rule unwittingly (they haven't read their bible) and are usually punished on the spot by penalty points or disqualification. This is reasonable justice and has an educational effect on the culprit. When it comes to paying green fees - that is a whole different ball game.
The green keeper at my club tells me he could write a book on the subject of fee dodgers - perhaps he should.

Ours is a small club and often unmanned. Visitors are 'on trust' to deposit the required fee into an envelope and post it into a secure box. On one occasion he arrived to find the car park full and a whole 'golfing society' were conducting a tournament without a single green fee having been paid. These were people who no doubt were applying the Rules of Golf to the letter whilst playing the game yet abusing the trust of the club hosting their activities. Not playing the game in fact.

Very often he would encounter two people playing golf with only one golf bag and having paid only one fee (against a clearly stated rule).

"I'm not paying for him - he's only learning."

It's embarrassing enough to have to question someone regarding their honesty but often the response is hostile and abusive.

"How dare you . Do you think I look like the kind of person who wouldn't pay ?" bellowed the man who hadn't paid.

Another stated that he was going to pay on his way out. Perhaps I should say 'others' as that is a regular excuse..

Mr. 'I'm technically correct', declared, "I paid £12 on Monday and your sign clearly states,' Monday to Friday £12.' The sign has now been changed to include the words 'daily rate'. A fee which incidentally, generously allows access to the course for the whole day.

The greenkeeper recalled once spotting a rather beat up old van early one morning in the car park and admitted that because of its appearance he did view it with some suspicion. He could see the owners of the vehicle out on the course and went to check if the appropriate fee had been posted into the green fee box. The box itself had a bar inside which allowed envelopes to pass clearly through but restrained hands with light fingers from making withdrawals. There was indeed a fee containing envelope in the box but it had been bent over the security bar. Figuring that this was a clever ploy to be able to claim having paid if questioned yet be able to reimburse oneself if not, our hero removed the fee from the envelope and replaced it with toilet paper. Concealing himself from view he waited for the players to return. As suspected they furtively crept up to the box to reunite themselves with their money (or should I say the club's money) and departed with some haste - and their ill gotten toilet paper.

At the end of the day it is simply a matter of theft. Perhaps the R & A should add another rule which states that any golfer caught stealing from a golf club will result in disqualification from all other clubs.

Golf does try to police itself whenever possible via a letters of complaint regarding misdemeanours from one club secretary to another , and this can be quite effective.

Other forms of stealing from golf clubs are probably the same as from anywhere these days. This is an age when if it's not screwed down - it's fair game. It's also an age when if it is screwed down - it's also fair game. Heavy items such as benches and even grass cutting machinery can disappear overnight. Sand bunker rakes bunk off as regularly as errant schoolboys. At our club every single brass fitting on the course's water system was removed in one fell swoop. We used to have a large stone trough originally used for quenching the thirst of farm animals. The green keeper tried to move it one day via his mini tractor but it was too heavy so he left it for another day when he could add some counter weights at the back. It disappeared that very night. Why, is not a difficult question to answer as they are expensive items at any garden centre. How ? Well that's a question that's mystified him ever since.

The other year there was the debacle regarding some bloke who was jailed for retrieving golf balls from lakes without prior permission. This raised contentious questions regarding who actually owned the lost balls, trespass and what have you. I'm not offering any opinion on the subject other than to say it seems that golf is the fair game - and golf courses are obviously viewed by many, even golfers, in the same light.

Mediobogdvm. A Roman Fort situated by Lakeland's Hard Knott Pass.

Lakeland porridge

Mediobogdvm, I can reveal (unless you already know of it) is a Roman Fort in a rather remote area of South West Cumbria, known today by its more familiar title of Hard Knott Castle and situated just to the North of the Hard Knott Pass.

I've seen Roman ruins at various sites and 2000 years of British weather plus the fact that they offer a rather splendid supply of free, dressed stone for local building works has left most of them requiring a great deal of imagination, even with the aid of archaeologists drawings. Mostly you find yourself wandering around a few grassy mounds that indicate where the footings of a wall that 'once was', was and an information leaflet fills in the rather extensive gaps.

Like many people, I've driven over the Hard Knott Pass on several occasions on my way to one fell walk or another, aware that there were some Roman ruins in the region but in too much of a hurry to bother. However, on one of these outings with my family, we thought we'd stop and picnic at the site of a Roman camp. Besides, the views across the Eskdale valley to the Scafell Mountains would make great background photographs. We parked in a small clearing just off the road and made our way up the grassy rise that hides from view one of Lakeland's most accessible but best kept secrets.

This is as an impressive a piece of Roman architecture as you'll find anywhere in Britannia. It is almost square with each wall measuring some 375 ft in length and standing about 6'6". The rounded lookout towers at each corner facing the points of the compass. The centre of each wall boasting a large gateway. Roman forts of this size and purpose were built to a standard plan with gateways set as described, regardless of the individual fort's situation. In this instance the NW gate opens to a dramatic drop over a precipice. Perhaps this was an elaborate back door for the Roman rubbish bins. It's hard to imagine any other practical use.

Granted, there has been some reconstruction of these walls by the Ministry of Works, but only using existing material, and in order to halt any further ravages of time. Mediobogdvm's location must have saved it from becoming incorporated into part of anything but a few local farms. Any buildings that were within these impressive walls would have been constructed of wood and only the usual low footings remain.
Away from the fort are the very depleted ruins of a small

Roman bathhouse and testament to Roman civil engineering skills is a levelled parade ground the size of the camp itself. You can also view the fort from the summit of nearby Harter Fell overlooking the Hard Knott Pass from its Southern flank and although it is a modest 2140 ft it commands a wonderful 360 degree view of the surrounding fells apart from its raven's eye view of Mediobogdvm. Any fell walker enjoying this viewpoint can imagine a Roman sentry on lookout duty standing on the very same spot.

From Harter Fell you get a good perspective on how the fort held a strategic position in the landscape. It also affords an entertaining view of motorists negotiating the twisting hairpin inclines of the pass. The fort itself has had its ups and downs, literally, having been sacked, burnt, abandoned and rebuilt during its years of service. It is believed to have been originally created during the first century on the orders of Agricola on his push Northwards and used to protect the trade route from the coastal fort at Glannaventa (Ravenglass) to Galava (Ambleside).

An inscription plaque found by the NE gate reads - For the Emperor Caesar Tragan Augustus, son of the divine Tragan, Conqueror of Parthia, grandson of the divine Nerva, Pontifex Maximum, Thrice Consul, The Fourth Cohort of Dalmatians.

All this pomp and majesty doesn't disguise the fact that this was a desolate place, the rear end of the Roman Empire. A place where I suspect any Roman soldier, whatever rank, didn't get posted to on merit and where unruly Roman soldiers did the equivalent of porridge.
The bath house is far too small for 500 squadies, more likely they were marched down from their huge parade

ground and into the freezing River Esk. Probably via the NE gate and down the precipice. Any Roman going AWOL here would have to face the local Brigant tribes who's main aim in life was to defeat the forces of occupation and lead themselves into the dark ages.

I could be entirely wrong with my assumptions. The camp at Mediobogdvm could have been regarded by all who spent time there as a sort of Butlinium Maximus.

Grey pedle power.

Last year I went to a party to celebrate an old art school friend's seventieth year. He'd treated himself to a new carbon fibre racing bike and having a passion for bikes myself I naturally inspected his new pride and joy. It weighed in at just fifteen pounds, which to you and I is roughly three bags of potatoes from the supermarket. Pretty light (for a bike). Most people are at least that amount overweight. Pretty heavy (for anyone). Not so my friend and his veteran cycling club mates. They were all there drinking his good health each of them bursting with health themselves. To a man, lean and bronzed, a tanned effect emphasised by white hair. When you see them cycling they sport calves and thighs like snooker table legs.

Their fitness is the product of years of exercise, to try and match them now would be almost impossible. Most of them have been cycling since being teenagers. Keen as I am on cycling I wouldn't attempt to stay with these chaps on a day out in on the Lancashire –Yorkshire roads, they would be out of sight within minutes. These aging athletes still enter time trials and veteran events. With an n average age of sixty plus they will regularly knock out over sixty miles. You've probably guessed, I'm impressed – and slightly envious.

These cycling fellows are very conscious and proud of their fitness. My birthday friend was telling me he had just been in hospital for a glaucoma test. As he had to go from one part of the hospital to a treatment room down stairs he was instructed to sit in a wheel chair, a porter would take him. He was most put out. "I've been round the Trough of Bowland on my bike this morning, I'm not sitting in that." His protests were ignored. I told him the request was probably a policy created from some fear of litigation. When he returned to his room he insisted he walk at the side of the porter and his wheel chair.

The wife of one of these aging athletes told me her husband had recently cycled from Lands End to John O'Groats. This imediately caught my interest as I have some pension aged friends who had also completed this journey. One with his wife on a tandem. I think they spent a couple of weeks, breaking the journey in hotels en route. I turned to the fellow, a slight chap with the usual bronzed complexion and aerodynamic nose, which is a common feature of these cycling types, they appear to be designed for speed. 'How long did it take you?' His reply stunned me. This was a fellow in his seventies, and one who had recovered from prostate cancer some years previously. 'Four days.'

I'll be the first to admit that mental arithmetic is not my forte, but I can work out quite quickly that the distance involved is roughly one thousand miles and divided by four leaves any potential cyclist about two hundred a fifly miles a day. I enquired how he had broken this down and I was answered in a matter of fact way. 'Lands End to Bristol, Bristol to Great Eccleston (his home near Blackpool) then two days to John O'Groats.' Further questioning revealed that he had spent some eighteen hours a day in the saddle.

My birthday friend simply said , 'Oh he's an animal, club champion for several years.' I'm sill stunned. Driving a car from Bristol to Blackpool is enough for me when I visit my daughter, and that's on a motorway.

My passion for bikes is slightly out of hand. At the last count I had five, plus two ladies shopping bikes at my caravan for tootling about. I can't justify having five of them, (or even seven) even though I'm asked to on a regular basis by my wife. They just accumulate. Bargains mainly. I'd certainly save even more money if I hadn't bought some of them. I will have a clear out soon.

Two of these are mountain bikes, which I occasionally take out (not both together –one will have to go) on the Pennine Fells or Forest trails in the Lakes. Even on the fell tops when I'm feeling fit. I often venture out with a couple of chaps who are in their seventies. I'm just a lad really not having quite reached septuagenarian status. A few months ago we did a bike ride known as the Salter Fell trail. This follows an old Roman road in part and crosses the fells from near Wray in the Lune Valley down to Slaidburn some eighteen kilometres away. Then back again by roads across the fells to where we parked our car. The road is a little easier although quite hilly in parts. Unlike my cycling friend, if the hill becomes too steep, I will get off and walk.

The other year one of the fellows I normally cycle with, bought himself a new American mountain bike - we retired people do indulge ourselves. Remember those three speed Sturmey Archer gears we used to have as boys? Today's machines come with up to twenty eight. On encountering his first steep incline he refused to dismount. After all, why have all these wall climbing gears if you're not going to use them? I waked beside him explaining that he was expending more energy than myself for the same result. He persisted in his endeavours, his peddles turning like a Kenwood mixer. I pointed out a feature at the top of the rise and made a bet that I would reach it first by simply walking. He gasped his acceptance of the point and joined me.

Birthday boy however, wouldn't even think about dismounting. He would simply have raced up it. Although over the years he knew most of the roads in the North of England, he had never done this thirty mile route over the fells and said he would join us next time we did it, telling us he would meet us where we parked our car. It takes the edge off one's sense of achievement when one of the party has cycled some twenty odd miles to the start point, and again after the ride, to cycle the same back home. At least it should take some of the sting out of his legs. He will have to cycle at our pace too, unless he wants to eat his sandwiches on his own.

The two chaps I cycle with are both extremely active fellows. They put me to shame. Both are keen para gliders and hang gliders and one is an avid skier. They even travel abroad to pursue these activities. There is a whole swath or these active Oldies about these days. Any reader who is maybe feeling a bit house bound or jaded could well do to check out some local clubs. The hills are alive with the sounds of pensioners. If your knees are dodgy you could paddle a canoe, sail or even take up golf. There are numerous activities out there, but I would recommend a bike every time. If you are concerned about traffic, try a canal towpath. No hills there. I know of one seventy odd year old who travelled virtually the length of England from Lancashire to London on his bike via canal towpaths. You could do the same right through France.

It's grey power – and it's green.

"It's rigor mortice, he died last night on the stairs!"

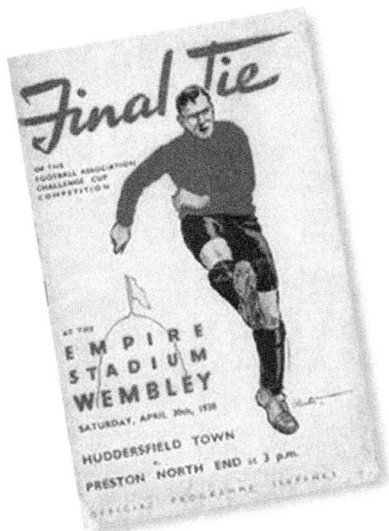

Up for the Cup - and flying caps.

It's hard to believe that the first televised FA Cup Final was in 1938.

I don't think there was a single television set in either of the two finalist's northern mill towns of Preston and Huddersfield, the word television wasn't even in their vocabulary, The first set I saw in Preston was in the 50s – and that was in a shop window. On the other hand, probably every single radio set in both towns was tuned in to the BBC Radio commentary.

Back in 1938 it was football's golden age. Capacity crowds filled every stadium and players, often earning less than £20 a week, were idolized. Production performance of local industries could be correlated with the success (or lack of it) achieved by a town's football club. The FA Cup Final at

Wembley Stadium was the Mecca for every team, and every street, workshop, mill and office would be represented by thousands of supporters making their way south by coach and rail to support them. Even my mother made the trip although she was hardly a regular football supporter. She'd gone along with my father who'd managed to get two tickets.

Amongst my late mother's effects I came across the FA Cup programme and half a ticket signed by the whole Preston Team for that glorious day. How my father had managed to acquire such a prize I'll never know. Bill Shankly, then a young Preston player was probably the most famous signature on the ticket but in 1938 most of the players on both teams were household names, at least in the football world.

Preston North End had reached Wembley the previous year only to be defeated in the final and Huddersfield Town had met Preston in the final of 1922. Huddersfield had won on a penalty 1 – 0 so there was a score to be settled and the pain of losing the previous year to be erased.

My mother told me that it was quite an experience just being there despite finding herself positioned right behind one of the goals and her view obscured. The game went into thirty minutes of extra time, and following another twenty-nine goal-less minutes the radio commentator Thomas Woodrooffe declared, "If anyone scores I'll eat my hat".

Quite a risky promise unless you are partial to an unfilled felt pasty. Seconds later the stadium was stunned and Mr Woodrooffe's trilby was on the menu when the referee blew his whistle awarding a penalty to Preston.

The elected penalty taker for Preston was George Mutch. For George, this was a chance to win Cup Medals for his team, glory for the thousands of supporters who'd made their way down the country and thousands more in Preston itself . This was also a clash between Lancashire and Yorkshire. Two sporting rival counties where the famous quote attributed to Bill Shankly rang true. 'Football isn't a matter of life and death – It's more important than that.'

George glanced toward the goal. If he'd peered through the netting he would have seen my mother with her eyes firmly closed. She couldn't watch. He was going to belt that ball straight down the centre with such power that it would need a quick hand and a strong arm to hold it even if the goalkeeper managed to get a touch. The keeper himself had decided that he would dive to his right.

Incredible press photo of the ball hitting the underside of the bar.

He made his move toward the ball. My mother's eyes were still firmly closed, peeping now could be bad luck. The whole of Wembley fell silent, George's heart must have skipped a beat, he'd struck it true but it was rising. The keeper was now horizontal to the ground and the ball was flying in a dead straight line for the crossbar. In a vain attempt the keeper flung an arm upwards but it was out of reach. It struck the underside of the bar picking up a line of fresh white paint as it then bounced down into the back of the net.

The Preston supporter's end of Wembley erupted along with the thousands of joyful fans around their radios. The chap standing next to my mother said to her in a broad Preston dialect, " Tha can open thi eyes now lass.– Ee's bloody scored!" To achieve the full poetic effect of his accent you must pronounce the 'o' in open as the 'o' in pop. Opening her eyes she recalled seeing thousands of Lancashire working men's caps being hurled aloft. When they fell back they were flung up again on mass. I don't think any Preston supporter returned home with his own cap that day.

On that subject I'm informed that Thomas Woodrooffe did keep his word.

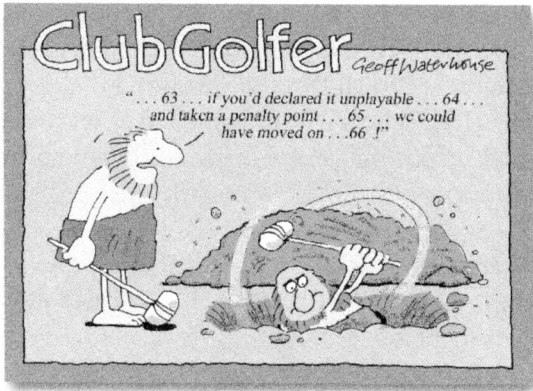

Postcard from the GoKart Electric golf trolley series.

A storm in a teapot.

A couple of years ago the golf club vice captain took me to one side and asked if I would be interested in becoming his vice captain the following year. Something of a shock really. I'm not the sort of bloke you would expect to take on the mantle of eventual captaincy. I'm a bit too laid back, or worse, slightly irreverent toward the club's hierarchy. Golf to me is just a game.

Over the preceding two years I had been cautioned for practising from the white (competition) tees. I'd wanted to check out the distance I could attain with a new club and as I struck the ball the club secretary popped out from behind a tree. I'd been caught in the act by the course police. Later I was admonished for selling golf balls at cut price to club members. This was deemed as converting the temple of golf into a market place. Shades of Jesus here, and too much for the high priests.

I'd had my fill of club committees from my involvement with another sport. As captain I would have to chair the club committee – and all that goes with it. I'd always been quite happy to let others get on with all that malarkey – and never complained if they came up with something I didn't particularly agree with (well not much).

But I was flattered. A fatal emotion. I did respond by saying I would think it over – and to this end I decided to conduct a discreet straw poll.

During the next competition day whilst down in a quiet corner of the course with my two playing partners. I confided in them regarding the proposal I'd received, adding that I didn't really think I was 'captain of a golf club' material. They both laughed and concurred with my assessment.

I instantly curtailed my straw poll on the grounds that I would probably receive much of the same from other players – but on a positive note I figured that from a position of such low expectation, it would be hard to fail.

Eventually, having considered the fact that I would be in my seventies and the chances were, that I wouldn't be asked again, I accepted. I then spent the next year as vice captain, looking and learning – and doing as little as possible.

At committee meetings I observed the general bickering between the male and female members. The main bone of contention being an on-going dispute which had rumbled on over several years, regarding the ladies making tea for their competition visitors via a kettle and a tea pot!

This contravened a long established club rule that forbids members from consuming their own food on club premises. I must point out that ours is a small club with no catering facilities – but we do have a tea/coffee machine. It was this perceived loss of revenue from this vending machine which was causing all the fuss.

The ladies argued that tea from a tea pot was a reciprocal arrangement for visiting club ladies. They presented tea from a teapot with their sandwiches and cakes rather than asking their guests to use the vending machine. This seemed reasonable enough for me and figured when I was captain I would formulate a final solution to the teapot problem. I didn't allow for the fact that I was entering a gender war that had been rumbling for decades. Obviously there was another gender-based agenda going on here – the teapot was just a catalyst. I was to become the golf club's Chamberlain advocating peace in our time.

Eventually the day came when I was to assume my position. Actually, the day came and nearly went as I'd assumed the A.G.M. was on a Sunday, but it was in fact on a Saturday and I had a phone call that evening asking where I was. They were about to install me as captain and I was fifty miles away watching television. I made it by the skin of my teeth, crept into the room full of assembled club members and took my place at the head of the table as the meeting was drawing to a close. As I sat down the captain declared that this was the point in the procedure that he would hand over his captaincy to the new captain – and I had to stand up again.

There are only two ways you can handle embarrassing situations. You can become embarrassed – or you can already be embarrassed. I chose the latter. I decided to use humour to wriggle out of the situation I had dropped myself in and told the members that they could refer to me as the 'late' captain. This seemed to go down well enough so I added a few more self deprecating comments, even told them about my failed straw poll. A member told me later that I'd managed against all odds to get away with it. I also said that I would try to ensure that I would do all in my power to keep the club as a 'friendly' club and to ensure good relations between the sexes.

Somewhat naively, I was about to enter a war zone.

My first committee meetings came and went. I was getting the hang of it. Being assertive when it was required and not leaving anything 'in the air'. When something required being attended to, I made sure that someone was charged with attending to it – before the next meeting. Simple. There was one monthly item though which regularly reared its silly head. The tea pot saga. Some male members on the committee were telling me that people were ready to resign over the issue. The lady members were also telling me that some of their members were thinking likewise. The sorry affair rumbled on, and on. Every time I entered the club someone was talking about teapots. You wouldn't believe adults could be so steamed–up regarding the use of a kettle.

After six months of this childish behaviour I decided that enough was enough and wrote a long-winded letter to the committee about the nonsense I had to put up with. I not only added this to 'any other business' but also into 'correspondence'. This ensured that the committee had to sit there whilst it was read out. It concluded telling them that I'd never aspired to follow my mother in the role of schoolteacher– but I'd inadvertently taken on this mantle as captain of this club. I even added I was looking forward to the end of term.

I then appealed for a compromise agreement and like a group of chastised children they then voted on a solution, which agreed to the use of the kettle on six occasions. I know, just six brews – but it was an agreement which some had said was impossible.

It was. The truce lasted about two weeks.

It then transpired that someone had kept a tally on the kettle use and the ladies had already overstepped the 'six' brews armistice. The news swept through the club and we were back to revolution and threats of resignations.

At the next month's meeting I again appealed for a line to be drawn under this affair. I organised a sub- committee to draw up another possible compromise solution to this rather childish problem. This was to be presented at the following month's meeting. Unfortunately I had to chair this heated committee, which went over all the well-covered tedious nonsense. Eventually I came up with an agreement which involved the donation of some money from the ladies section to cover the perceived loss of revenue and a new agreed number of occasions from six, up to fourteen times when the offending teapot would be utilised.

Hooray. War had been averted. Again.

This proposal was voted through at the next committee meeting. My heroic efforts had established peace on the western front. The tea wars were over and my year in office would be heralded as the stuff of history.

However, at the same meeting it was pointed out that there had been another drinks related problem. A shortfall of money from the tea/coffee machine due to some members not paying. This was normally dispensed on 'trust' and the cash either put in an envelope or paid over the bar, when open. It was hastily decided to put the drink sachets behind the bar until a coin operated sachet dispenser could be installed.

Less than a week later some ladies at the club, claiming they didn't have a key for the bar – decided to put the kettle on. As a reprisal, an insurgent then later locked the electric kettle in a cupboard and subsequently the ladies couldn't make tea for their visitors the following week. Oh no!!!

There's another brewing storm brewing that I'm going to have to defuse.

As if golf isn't a silly enough game already.

Don't mention the War

The Mulberry floating harbour is a monument to ingenuity and creative thinking. Without it, I would probably be typing this in German. Those huge concrete caissons, now barnacle covered, listing and home to crabs and the like – are still a dominant landmark (if you can have such a thing at sea), and a most impressive sight when viewed from the beaches. Echoes of D Day dominate the area and most visitors are there, simply to stand where so many had fallen. Like so many theatres of war, It remains locked into its past.

I sailed on those very beaches a few years ago, when the European Sand Yacht Championships were held at the little town of Asnelle. At low tide we were sailing with our racecourse just a few yards from the harbour itself. It was quite incongruous really. Here we were, English and German sailors racing on the arena where some of our fathers had been engaged in a desperate life and death struggle. A German competitor who I knew quite well, told me he had lost the father he had never really known during the D Day landings We had both been infants at the time.

Any sporting event involving England and Germany has a certain extra edge to it. In our sport 'fighting them on the beaches' takes on a whole new meaning. It's all done in good humour and the Germans themselves recognise this rather silly extra dimension to the game. At Dunkirk we had a German fellow called Thomas who had earned his place in the British team whilst working in the UK for a year. I presented Thomas with a WW2 helmet with the name Tommy imprinted on it. "The last Tommy to wear this," I told him, "was on this very beach!"

The Championships are held in a different country each year and the host club organises a social programme for competitors during the weeklong event. Whilst at Asnelle we were invited to visit a cinema at Arromanches dedicated to the D Day landings. It's a remarkable building housing a 360-degree cinema screen. The audience stands in the centre and the back projected cine films, featuring black and white newsreel footage along with war correspondents archive material are being projected all around you. You can look out to sea and witness the naval guns bombarding the German defences. The shells and tracer bullets can be heard whistling overhead and as you turn you see and hear the shoreline buildings exploding and shattering. We were transported not just back in time – but on to the Normandy D Day beach we had just been racing on.

Our visit to the cinema was by coach and our French guide was a fellow competitor, Veronique, who we all knew from years in the sport. Most of us on the coach had sailed together over the years at various European events and had built up strong friendships. Veronique was herself a Champion and a popular figure in the sport. She spoke in English, which is just as well as my French, is less than poor despite my many visits. Veronique gestured out to the Mulberry Harbour and speaking with a voice full of emotion she said, "This is where the wonderful Allies landed to save us from the". . . there was a slight pause and a flicker of panic froze on her face for a microsecond as she remembered that the coach was half full of Germans. We all realised she was in a deep hole with no obvious way out. Then with a nervous smile she continued. . . . "from the wonderful Germans."

By a moment of inspired diplomacy Veronique had avoided
World War 111 and the whole coach erupted in laughter
and applause.

Sporting whites

Unfortunately my inherited genes have granted me custody
of a pair of lower limbs that although enabling me to be
fleet of foot, do have the appearance of another species.
My drumstick muscular calves bulge quite high at the top
and taper dramatically down to slender feminine ankles.
Their whiteness, also a genetic feature, is almost equalled
by this page. How I envy those who can strut around the
fells or on the sports field with oaken legs that declare their
owners as true outdoor creatures.

I do endeavour each year , during our all too brief
summers, to try to give them some semblance of a tan, but
to no avail. Although I feel the sun's rays being absorbed as
I potter around the garden - the fact is, that the rays are
being reflected back to their source by the sheer whiteness.

I did once manage to impart some colour into them having
spent a full day in an open canoe. Not oaken legs though,
not even light oak. No, freshly boiled lobster was more the
hue. The cerise glow declaring a visual warning, the very

colour of pain itself. I slid into bed that night very quickly lest my wife should detect my new radiating limbs and admonish me for obvious stupidity. I lay
sleepless throughout the night with two uncovered radiator bars for legs, warming the whole room.

The very next day we were at a wedding reception and I tried to act as normally as I could with two swollen, oversized and overdone, splitting sausages down each leg of my trousers. " I don't feel too good," I explained, as an excuse from dancing and mingling. Later my wife returned to our table and decided to sit on my lap.

I withstood the ensuing pain as well as any victim of the Gestapo. You could take a blow lamp to my limbs and my comrades would be safe. However,the pressure did nothing to help the cooking sausages. It was as though my trousers were now a size too small. I was a candidate for hospital treatment, but embarrassment forbade such action. It was several days before my wife discovered the extent of my stupidity and folly - she was never slow at speaking her mind.

I suffered so for several weeks as my swollen legs peeled, wept and stung till at last returning to their normal, blanched, abnormal state. Lobster thermidor is now off the menu with liberal applications of my grandchildren's factor 25 I discovered left in the bathroom cabinet.

It was following one bright, sunny day busying myself around our caravan that I retired for the evening sensing a satisfactory, tingling warmth to my legs - and checking them in the mirror, through oak tinted specs, I convinced myself that they were at least 'off white'. Tinted enough, I figured , to be put on public display despite their shape. And so, with a new air of confidence, the morrow found me stepping to the first tee on the golf course in sporty looking shorts.

I looked down at my new found oak tree legs as I fired a ball up the centre of the fairway and strode out after it with some style.

It's amazing what tricks the brain can play on willing eyes. I soon realised that my single day's previous exposure to the sun had done little to enhance the appearance of my legs. They were still white to all but myself.   Persil white.

Forget all that stuff about golf being a ' good walk spoilt' - the golf course is where you get to know yourself, and others. It is the venue for great humour, wit, pathos, and despite the proclaimed rules of etiquette, comments on players conduct, ability and appearance fly with wonderful banter. The golf course is no place for the faint hearted. You give it, and take it, in equal measure.

It is to my fourball mates great credit that they contained themselves for a good three holes before one of them commented on my new sporty look. As I steadied myself for a drive an amused voice declared, "The last time I saw legs like that - they were being served with stuffing, gravy and two veg." Before the initial laughter had subsided, another added, "You should have sent them back - they weren't done!"

Remember, remember . . .

You are probably aware of my incendiary interest from previous admissions of my flirtations with flame (little piece about being an infant fire starter). Bonfires always held a fascination for me throughout my childhood – but thankfully not beyond. November the fifth was always a highlight date, not just for myself, but the event was a big affair for all the young lads in my village. Planning started weeks before this.

There were probably three or four major bonfires in the area. I'm not counting all the mini private ones. I'm talking about the twenty-foot monsters that just grew and grew. The kids in neighbourhood scuttled back and forth like leaf cutter ants carrying and dragging branches, old furniture, fence posts – in fact anything made of wood, or indeed that hopefully would burn.

Raids were made on each other's stockpiles, the bonfires themselves were not constructed properly till the final days or hours lest the competition should prematurely ignite it. Guards were mounted prior to countdown – it was a serious business. Pride was at stake.

At ignition time, some parents decided to get involved under the guise of responsibility. They'd watched the fuel stocks grow and grow and wanted part of the action. They would add the extra muscle required for construction and provide the petrol for lift –off.

Guy Fawkes was meanwhile being prepared to meet his maker. He wore an old suit filled with straw, not unlike

Worzel Gummage, and always wore a trilby as I recall. There were plenty of trilbies about in the 40s and even in the 50s. You'd be hard pushed to find one these days but you can probably buy a Chinese made, Guy Fawkes kit made of plastic in Tescos, complete with face mask and tall black hat to help you be creative.

Firework stockpiles were also growing, every child had his own personal stash converted from pocket money and cash collected from returning empty pop bottles. In the 40s and 50s there were two major firework manufacturers, Brocks and Standard. I seem to recall another called Payne's but they never figured in my reckoning. The Roman Candles, Volcanoes, Snowstorms, Chrysanthemum Fountains and Catherine Wheels were fine, but for us boys it was the bangers that ruled. Bangers, flip-flaps and rockets. I remember one; I think it was a spitfire, a banger with little cardboard wings. It was in effect a self-destructing jet plane but it was early days for jet-powered craft, otherwise it would have had a more jet inspired title. Doodlebug would have been a tad insensitive.

As ten (ish) year olds we would wander the streets from bonfire to bonfire with pockets bulging with bangers collected over the preceding weeks. Mighty Atoms, Little Demons, Cannons, Squibs each one had its distinctive blast and each one of us a potential Guy Fawkes. A spark away from oblivion.

Bangers on their own were ok, but it's what you could do with them. You could light the touch paper and not throw it till it had begun to fizz – like a junior hand grenade. Luckily, most of us have retained our hands. They could be placed on people's doorsteps as a variation on the old 'knock and run'. A favourite was to explode them in biscuit tins and watch the lids fly into the air – or tie them to rockets to create flying bombs. Rockets themselves were much more fun sent horizontally down the street, perhaps with flip-flaps tied to them for extra directional mayhem.

The current lobby against fireworks is more than justified. Fireworks are dangerous, how we were ever allowed such freedom is unbelievable. Kids are totally irresponsible. We certainly were, and I'm sure today's youngsters are no different than us.

These days, bonfire night is still held to celebrate the burning of poor old Mr Fawkes. His effigy still sits in pride of place at the centre of things as he has for hundreds of years. Perhaps we'd still be setting him ablaze if he'd been successful in his mission. He was destined for immortality. Something of an irony, staying alive by being burnt over and over.

Firework displays are now rather splendid affairs with huge expensive devices made in China. Responsible folk keep the children in safe areas and everyone is plied with treacle toffee and baked potatoes. When my children were little, we were invited to a neighbour's house to one such organised affair. The children were all safe and sound inside the house watching the fireworks through the patio windows. Each firework was given an introduction and individually ignited. That was, until a spark from one landed in the tin holding the arsenal and the whole lot went up together. Fantastic. Remember, remember, the fifth of November . . . those kids certainly will.

Leyland tanks and Lancaster bombers.

A roadside display just outside Leyland features a WW2 tank with a plaque proudly declaring 'Made in Leyland'. As I drive past I like to think that my father was possibly involved in creating that very tank. During the war years he'd worked at Leyland Motors. He did tell me that he had wanted to join the Navy but being an engineer it was a 'reserved occupation'.

Actually, I didn't even realize they made tanks there until he'd retired from being an engineer to buy a small news agency. To mark the occasion the company presented him with a certificate recording that he'd spent twenty-five years there, as if he didn't know. Management individuals would probably have received a clock, a gold watch or even a golden handshake, but highly skilled engineers from the shop floor only merited a certificate, albeit with a colourful border featuring Leyland buses, trucks – and a Cromwell tank.

Cromwell tank in Normandy.

The Cromwell A27 Cruiser tank was built by Leyland from 1943 and saw its first action in Normandy in 1944. It was popular with its crews due to its speed, mind you, it needed to be quick because it was out gunned by its foe, the German Tiger tank which also boasted armour the Cromwell couldn't penetrate. It was however, very effective against other armoured vehicles.

I was born in January 1941. Not an ideal time to bring a child into the world, but Penwortham was a world away from any wartime dangers. In fact the only couple of actions my father witnessed was a single bomb dropped by a German bomber on its way back from a raid on Liverpool onto his Leyland Motors' workshop. Luckily it failed to explode and lodged in the roof girders - the evacuation drill at the factory was achieved in record time.

His other experience was when another returning Luftwaffe pilot shed his remaining bombs on the nearby Longton marshes. My father, hearing the explosions, opened the front door – only to be thrown backwards down the hall by a blast of air from the final bomb.

When you consider that just thirty miles away in both Liverpool and Manchester, the full horrors of war were being felt by civilians, yet our lives were hardly touched. We did have a couple of evacuees living with us and obviously we had to endure rationing but generally we were lucky.

My father kept bees and the resulting honey was used to barter for other items. It was a general support system that I think the authorities turned a blind eye to. This 'black (ish) market' probably fell under the umbrella of 'Digging for Victory'. Fresh eggs were available from the local farm along with other rationed items. Rabbits supplemented meat rations and so village life went on much as before. Once my father was asked to deliver a sack of contraband hams to an address in the village. Fortunately it was a time of 'blackout' and he furtively made his nervous way in the shadows arriving relieved and unchallenged at his destination. The recipient emptied the sack on to the kitchen table and pointing to each item in turn he said, "This one is for the Police Sergeant, this one for Councilor Jones, this is the Vicar's ". . . and so on.

My own contribution to the war effort was as a four-year old unofficial war artist. Armed only with pencil and paper I was responsible for dismantling vast quantities of the German war machine. I can recall drawing what would pass as a Lancaster bomber with its telltale fins on the tail plane and large bulbous gun turrets bristling with machine guns.

These drawings would be accompanied by my audible 'ack, ack, ack' sound as they fired a dotted pencil line of bullets at German fighters, each denoted by a bold black cross. My sound effects grew louder as each fighter was hit and sent spiralling down to the foot of the paper in a frenzied scribble of pencil smoke. Then, a huge explosion would be heard as my mission was completed. Anti-aircraft guns were also in my armoury and I brought down whole squadrons of Luftwaffe bombers.

Incidentally, the Lancaster bomber wasn't actually made in Lancaster, but they were still made in Lancashire. It was a successor to the 'Manchester' bomber and most of all Lancasters in wartime were manufactured at Chadderton near Oldham.

My imaginary war effort included tanks, but my tanks were invincible against any tank the Germans could offer. Oddly enough, they never fired back and my pencil shells would make noisy direct hits every time. In my four-year old's world, war was just another game.

Waterhouse.

Postcard from the GoKart Electric golf trolley series.

A Froggy day in Loch Lomond

A visit to the home of the Scottish Open

Let me start this little piece by telling you that I am a very average golfer. My style is evidently self taught and drastically unorthodox. My clubs are a strange collection of shortened irons, a lengthened driver and a few assorted chippers and rescue clubs.

There is one club amongst this ensemble which I use time and again, its name, given by its American manufacturer is a Slippery Frog. Why a Slippery Frog? I've no idea, but it even has this title and a frog engraved on the sole of the club.

The Slippery Frog was designed to emulate the greenside game using a three wood by Tiger Woods. It has a three wood head and a putter shaft and I find it reasonably accurate from about 150 yards. Accurate enough to get my handicap down to 14, which isn't so bad considering I only took up the game at sixty.

Being captain elect at my own little club in the Lakes I decided to approach Britain's most exclusive club, Loch Lomond, to try and arrange a game via the visiting captains courtesy scheme, which most clubs endorse. With a possible successful outcome I emailed Sandy, a lady whose company, GoKart I do cartoons for, to ask if she would be my guest. Both she and her husband Chris, both ex professionals, had failed in their attempts to play there despite also being manufacturers of one of Britain's leading electric golf trolleys.

The secretary of the club replied promptly and negatively. He did explain that he was only following his members' wishes that the course should not be open to non-members. I can't really blame them. At a joining fee of £55,000 I wouldn't want the likes of myself on the course!

Just a few weeks following my failed attempt I had an email from Sandy who had just purchased a four-ball for a golf competition at an auction run by a children's charity called SPARKS – and the venue incredibly was the Loch Lomond club, home of the Scottish Open. The game would be followed by a gala dinner and a night at the Loch Lomond Clubhouse. Was I interested !!?

I had to find a guest from my own club and asked a friend called Alan who I often play in competitions with, if he would care to join us. Silly question really. Any golfer in the world would jump at the chance.

Originally, as the game was to be played on a Monday and I asked if it could be arranged for us to stay there on the Sunday night. I changed my mind when I discovered that staying the extra night there would have cost us £400. We decided to stay at a B&B over a chip shop in Balloch at the foot of the Loch, and meet our hosts on Monday morning.

Driving up to the clubhouse through the parkland course was scenic splendour itself. Manicured fairways and mature trees with the Loch beyond. Then we came across the clubhouse. Rossdhu House, a palatial Georgian country house originally built by the Clan Colquhoun, its double columned portal gained by a sweeping stone staircase up to the first floor, and the whole splendid edifice commanding stunning views over the lawns to the Loch.

The Loch Lomond club for all its grandeur was reputed to have lost about 5 million pounds last year alone. There was talk of it being taken over by a hotel group and also a possible buy-out by members to keep it exclusive. Staff members and an army of green keepers were everywhere. No wonder the place was leaking money. I parked my humble Picasso in front of the magnificent clubhouse and a black clad attendant rushed to open my door asking for my keys. 'I'll just take your car round to your lodge sir,' he declared holding out his hand. A hand which I later realised was also expecting a crisp Scottish Fiver. I declined his invitation telling him that I would deliver it myself following registration. Giving a rather disparaging look at my Picasso he remarked, 'don't think you're leaving that here all day.' Cheeky sod, he had a trace of a cockney accent too. It wasn't like he was a son of the Colquhoun Clan.

As he spoke, the distant rumble of an approaching member in a Masseratti cruised in and parked alongside my Citroen. The lackey swooped to open his door and fawned his way into the club with the member's bags. A Masseratti, that would probably register a twenty on the tip scale. We were left to make our entrance up the sweeping stairs to register.

Our slightly over-the-top lodge was possibly a six star affair with two huge canopied beds and thick goose downed duvets, each massive bed standing some three-foot above the tartan patterned carpet. Alan asked if I would need any help getting on to it. A tartan painted cupboard between the beds boasted a decanter of 15-year-old malt for the guests use. I don't drink the stuff myself but Alan made good use of it. The interior designer had been obviously briefed to make sure any American guests knew they were in Bonny Scotland. The wallpaper was tartan and even the painted wardrobes.

We met Sandy and Chris at breakfast before venturing out to the practice ground. You could probably fit a big section of our own little course in this area alone. Pyramids of practice balls were displayed for our use and competitors at each end were whacking balls like some military 'fire at will' command on an enemy outpost in the centre.

It was to be a shotgun start, so we made our way to our designated tee. Being a four-ball and each having a caddy was something I wasn't exactly looking forward to. For me, having a caddy was something of an embarrassment. I asked who had drawn the short straw and a fellow presented himself. It tuned out he played off one. This didn't help matters. Every time I made a shot I had an audience of seven. Two ex-pro golfers and five extremely low handicap players.

My first drive went well enough but just veered off the fairway. This despite the strange glances I was getting with regard to my unorthodox stance. I tend to place my right foot behind my left and swing from out to in. I have the appearance of facing the wrong direction. Christ, Alan,' I commented as we strode after our balls, 'these fairways are in better shape than our greens!'

I found my ball in fairly short rough about 140 yards from the green. My caddy was about to recommend a club until he inspected my bag of adulterated oddments. He hesitated, then asked me what I thought would do the trick. "I'll take the Frog, The Slippery Frog,' I said confidently.

The look on his face was fabulous. I wasn't going to take this course apart, but I decided I was going to have some fun. He handed me the club and I successfully launched it from the rough but it just skipped through the green.

The next hole was a bit longer and for my second shot I chose the Slippery Frog, and for my approach shot I told my caddy that perhaps the Slippery Frog would just the ticket. By now he was getting the idea and was soon suggesting that I used the Slippery Frog from fairway or rough. I don't normally rely on this club to that extent, but it is generally true and gets me out of trouble. I wasn't playing too well but at least I was getting round without too much trouble.

The course at Loch Lomond isn't that difficult for a steady golfer. What you see is what you get. There are no hidden traps or too much water. I admit I didn't play it very well but if I were to attempt it again, without a caddy, I would probably play to my handicap.

My caddy, having got used to the fact that his services were superfluous apart from carrying my bag, became quite relaxed and began relating some of his caddying experiences and an anecdote concerning one of his friends who was caddying for a four-ball some time ago.

There is a rather unkind golf expression (which I don't subscribe to, or use myself) it is used to describe a miscued shot, One that is not the best looking but runs like the clappers, They call it a Sally Gunnell.

The caddy he was talking about witnessed such a shot and blurted out, 'It's a bit of a Sally Gunnell.' Unfortunately the shot maker tuned out to be Sally's father.

The caddy didn't get a tip.

I gave my caddy twenty quid, I reckon he'd earned it.

Playing at Loch Lomond was a once in a lifetime experience. How many other golfers at club level can claim to have played there? I owe a real debt of thanks to my hosts. My friend Alan, playing with Chris came second and each won a crystal Champaign ice bucket with a silver band around and engraved with the Loch Lomond 'stag' logo. These were presented prior to the Gala Dinner. A fabulous result for Alan and our hosts.

Following the dinner was a charity auction where moneyed diners displayed their wealth bidding vast sums for donated items. The sponsor of the event was TAG HEUER, the watch manufacturer and they passed one of their watches around the room for inspection prior to being auctioned. It was a huge, multi-dialled wristwatch, a thing that will give you the time even if you happen to be diving near the Titanic. Or if you are in outer space it will give you the time in Tokyo, possibly even the current price of gold. The object went for about two and a half thousand pounds. My hands stayed locked under the table throughout. I don't need a TAG watch – I've got a LEGO one.

I'm disappointed that I didn't play as well as I can but I'm so grateful to my hosts for the experience. My Slippery Fog saved me from looking really stupid and my caddy learned something new.

It will be another tale for his next four ball.

"Can't you read?"

Vintage postcard of Hampsfell Hospice.

Hampsfell, a view with a room.

Grange over Sands is my favourite little seaside town, overlooking Morecambe Bay, sheltered from the North winds by Hampsfell and its sea warmed by the tail end of the Gulf Stream. The 'over-Sands' was added to differentiate it from the other Grange in Borrowdale for postal reasons (pre Post Code) though it would be more accurate to now add 'over Grass' due to the beach becoming something of a field over the last few years with salt marsh lambs grazing on its foreshore.

Never the less, it is a little town full of charm with delightful shops, an ornamental lake, home to a variety of exotic water birds, well kept gardens with a Victorian band-stand and several fine hotels for the visitors.

Well, that's my travelogue bit done, except to add that

Grange has two golf courses and is the perfect base for anyone who wishes to tour the Lake District. Actually, this very location is why we chose to have our caravan just outside Grange.

In 2001 access to the fells was interrupted by the foot and mouth epidemic which resulted in a total ban on fell walking, so I turned my attention to one of Granges two golf courses. I'd never played the game but the Grange Fell course on Hampsfell at least offered a chance to enjoy glorious panoramic views of Morecambe Bay and the Lakeland Fells as I hacked my way around.

I figured that the best way to pick up the game of golf was by osmosis, I'd watch and learn, and having been accepted as a member, I simply put my name down on the list for the next competition. This is not a recommended method. The three chaps who drew the short straws which resulted in having to play with me, deserve some praise for their patience. I scored twelve on the first par four hole. The rest of the round was a complete bogie-fest. What they didn't realize though, was my determination to succeed, and within just a few short years (and lots of practice) I had my handicap down to a respectable fourteen and won a few competitions on the way.

The foot and mouth epidemic continued for some time and the closure of the fells included Hampsfell. Any ball which strayed over the stone perimeter wall onto the fell was not just deemed out of bounds – but was irretrievable by law. This law however was obviously routinely ignored by deer, foxes, sheep, badgers, rabbits, kestrels, crows and whatever other wildlife chose to wander in and out. It's a wonder the epidemic was contained at all with this free movement of hooves, claws and paws throughout Lakeland.

Eventually we got the all clear and I would often wander up Hampsfell to the little tower at the summit known as the Hospice. Once I even took a wedge and chipped a golf ball all the way up to it, which does show what an easy little walk it is.

It was built in the mid 19th Century by the philanthropic Vicar of Cartmel as a refuge for walkers. It's a square limestone tower standing almost twenty feet tall and containing a single room with a fireplace. To gain an even better 360-degree view you can ascend to the flat roof via some very basic stone steps protruding from one outer wall, the only security being a flimsy wrought iron handrail. In the centre of the roof area there's a round table-like structure which has a revolving wooden pointer. By aligning this up with any distant feature you can discover what it is - from Blackpool Tower to most of the Lakeland Fells.

I think it fair to say that I got away with my year as Golf Captain. Both myself and the Club survived. I even managed to win the coveted North West Captain's Trophy at Ulverston Golf Club. Quite an achievement for someone who didn't start playing till he was sixty.

I don't play any more now, maybe I'll start again when my knees give out and I can't make it up the fells but I still call into Grange Fell Golf Club on my way to Hampfell's Hospice.

Uncle Frank's lobsters.

Being lucky enough to write this little column gives me the opportunity to write a few words about a man I knew as Uncle Frank, one of Blackpool's unsung entrepreneurs. He was one of those people who, over the decades, helped to keep Blackpool the UK's leading holiday resort, together with the theatre and fun fair owners, the tower and pier builders and all those who invested their money and their lives in the town they loved.

His name was Frank Vickers, not my real uncle, but the husband of my late mother's friend from their college days in the 1920s. Frank was an electrician by trade but a born businessman. My mother recalled how he'd once persuaded my father to act as his company secretary on a business trip to some Town Council in East Lancashire, where Frank had put in a successful tender for the removal of some slag heaps. He was a one-man band at the time but any businessman needed a company secretary at his side, if only for appearances. My mother told me, that Frank then sold back the slag heaps to another department of the same council who required hard core for a road-building project. Business is business.

His initial business venture in Blackpool was a successful enterprise, selling freezer units he'd developed which would convert any room into a cold store for the catering trade. He also had his own involvement in the industry with a fleet of 'stop me and buy one' ice cream trikes. His first restaurant however, became one of Blackpool's showpieces, The Lobster Pot on Market Street.

Back in the 1950s you would only see lobster on the menu at five star hotels – and even then at a price, but this was Blackpool, and as the rhyme says - 'noted for fresh air and fun'. This is the town where Mr. and Mrs. Ramsbottom could enjoy champagne on draught at Yate's Wine Lodge and order Lobster Thermidor at The Lobster Pot with bread and 'best' butter with a pot of tea. Its Menu from the 60s offers a whole lobster for just twelve shillings. The Ramsbottoms could even find themselves sitting at a table next to one of the town's show biz celebrities or a Cabinet Minister staying in Blackpool at Conference time.

The Lobster Pot was everyone's favourite.

 Having captured the public's imagination in his Lobster Pot, he opened the Café Royal, which overlooked the sea front. Here he installed a chicken rotisserie from the USA and had it positioned outside on the promenade. This was a time when chicken was still a luxury, only enjoyed on a Sunday, (if you were lucky). Visitors would stand and watch as chickens turned on their spits (very little on TV back then) and were able to take away a fresh, roast chicken in an insulated bag. This was unique to Blackpool.

Frank Vickers later purchased Jenkinson's Restaurant on Talbot Square and converted it into Blackpool's first Cabaret restaurant and nightclub, The Movenpic. I went there several times with my wife. Where else in any northern town could you enjoy a meal and a cabaret with topline acts of the day.

When I was a student in the 50s, Uncle Frank employed me one summer at his food preparation enterprise. This was a huge industrial building which housed a vast cold storage room with rows of crates containing frozen chickens from their own farm. All kinds of seafood and a mountain of frozen salmon. It was here I watched as they produced a Lancashire holidaymaker's favourite – black puddings. The main ingredient being a vat of coagulating pig's blood, which has resulted in my never, ever, wishing to taste black pudding.

I recall being served a halibut steak at The Lobster Pot almost the size of my plate, but up till then, I'd no idea just how big these fish actually were. As soon as they arrived fresh, we quickly had to transport them to the deep freeze unit at Fleetwood. Imagine trying to carry a seven stone, flat, wet, floppy halibut. The only way to grip them is by the gills before hoisting them over your shoulder. My day's work there would end with me smelling like a halibut.

Crabs and Lobsters were all cooked at this facility, prior to daily delivery to the restaurants. Their sharp claws were firmly taped up to avoid them gripping each other or snapping at the cooks' fingers. I also worked on the daily delivery vans, which gave me an insight into the sheer volume of seafood and chickens consumed in this popular Blackpool restaurant and nightclub chain.

Eventually, Frank sold his mini empire and retired as a tax exile to the Isle of Man where he ended his days happily. I think Blackpool is now ready for another Frank Vickers. . . . or two.

COMPLAINTS
↓

Waterhouse

A slection of Stott Park bobbins.

Turning things around.

Your grandma's friend Dolly was a household name throughout the UK. Actually, Dolly wasn't a real friend but more of a help to granny on washday in the days before washing powders could make your whites even whiter than white. Her full name was Dolly Blue and she was a little bag containing a block of 'blue' fabric whitener on a stick which granny would swish about in the final rinse of her washing to make her whites, well, if not whiter, at least a little less yellow.

The Dolly Blue factory was at Backbarrow near the foot of Windermere and closed in 1968, probably due to the afore mentioned whiter than white detergents and the home of the little blocks of whitener has now become a little block of apartments.

Dolly Blue fabric whitener.

I'd like to draw your attention though, to the little stick that protruded from Dolly's little bag. It was made just down the road in a little wood turning factory at Finsthwaite.

Stott Park bobbin mill had been established there in 1835 and could turn its hand, (or its wood), to a variety of wooden products apart from Dolly's little sticks. They made spout bobbins for the building trade, used as spacers when attaching drainpipes to walls. They also made handles for a variety of tools and even had a contract with the M.O.D. for supplying handles for stick grenades and toggles for naval duffle coats.

Its core business though, was making bobbins. Not just those little wooden ones on sewing machines, but a whole variety of industrial sized bobbins for Lancashire's cotton industry. Others were made for coiling wire. It's easy to imagine that this was some quaint 'cottage' industry, tucked away in the woods, but Stott Park was just one of over sixty Lakeland bobbin mills turning out between them tens of millions of bobbins every year. All this was from a sustainable source of coppiced wood. These woods are still part of the Lakeland landscape, but are no longer managed and are now overgrown.

In 1960, Stott Park's records show that it had purchased over 500 tons of coppice wood to add to its own local supply. The Lakeland mills were using a third of a million tons of wood each year. Sadly, the introduction of plastic bobbins together with the decline of the cotton industry caused a down turn and the eventual closure of all these turning mills. Stott Park was one of the last to go in 1971.

The mill then stood idle for a decade. Everything inside remained as it was, even to the tools being left on the benches. Fortunately its location within the village saved it from being vandalized or looted. Its biggest threat was from developers who looked to convert it into apartments like the ones at Dolly Blue.

Luckily, English Heritage was persuaded to step in and open it up as a working mill and visitor centre. It's a fascinating experience, discovering how bobbins were created from local wood and the guide there will take you through each stage as you wend your way through a path of knee high wooden shavings. You're accompanied by the clatter of the vintage machines, all driven by rows of leather belts festooned from the central drive shafts. It was here I discovered where the expression 'knocking off' came from. Apparently, when a factory workman was to leave his station for a break, he would clout the drive belt with a piece of wood to disengage his machine – hence 'knocking off'.

It's all quite safe of course for the visitors these days, but, we met an old chap who'd spent his whole working life at the mill. He told us that when he was a young lad, he'd caught his hand in a press. Not serious enough to lose his fingers (which was not unusual) but still extremely painful.

The foreman took him outside and plunged his hand into a bucket of cold water for half an hour – but then told him to return to work.

Those were the good old days!

The Stott Park water cure.

Stott Park Mill is well worth a visit. On one day a week they fire up the ancient steam engine, which was installed in 1880. It's hard to believe, that it they were still reliant on steam and later, water turbines until mains electricity eventually reached Stott Park mill as late as 1941.

At the end of your guided tour you can take home a newly created little bobbin memento and on a nice day you can also picnic at High Dam, a pretty tarn set in the woods, the original water source for Stott Park's 32' diameter water wheel (now long gone). It's a quiet, secluded spot, home to a variety of water birds just bobbin' about. Sorry, I can never resist a pun.

WW1 embroidered postcard.

Did you get my card ?

Having picked up a few old seaside postcards in France to decorate our salle de bain, I realise that the custom of sending such holiday souvenirs must be universal. There must have been millions of 'wish you were heres' going backwards and forwards around Europe since Victorian times.

Even today, when it seems everyone is in daily contact by mobile phone, the obligatory post card is sent back to the office or to friends and family. You risk being reprimanded if you don't. These days you expect to arrive home long before your card - that's all part of the accepted charm.

It's not the Post Office's fault; they now have a different roll to play. Important mail is delivered by fax or e-mail. Mr Postie now staggers up my path daily with an assorted pile of unsolicited brochures and news of yet another credit card opportunity. I'm not sure what it costs them, but The Readers Digest spend a small fortune telling me I'm a finalist (yet again) in their draw to win a fortune. This lucrative source of income for the Post Office puts the priority for the humble post card down the list.

There are postcards on every subject. I've even come across bizarre book that has a collection of Britain's most boring cards with dull views of some of the naffest 50's and 60's architecture. Stupendously awful shopping precincts and even car parks. Places that you wouldn't write home about are all there on a postcard for you to write home about.

Postcards seem to be one of those items that people don't discard (oops a pun) and get saved in a drawer for a lifetime. Eventually they may turn up during a house clearance and some will find there way into the hands of a dealer.

Most collectors' fairs have dealers selling old postcards. Apparently this is a huge business and there are fairs devoted entirely to selling old postcards. They even have their own magazine. The dealers tend to display older cards which are quite nostalgic and really entertaining. They are all classified by subject and have sections for various areas, counties, towns and villages. This is memory lane with an extra dimension. The views themselves are interesting but the real entertainment is reading the messages on the back. Well, they were never really private letters were they? They were written on an open card after all for the entire world to see. Not convinced eh! Well, when you next come across a few cards - just you try and resist reading a couple. Besides, that's all part of the fun. If you really don't like the idea then make sure you don't leave a pile of old postcards in a box somewhere, I may end up reading them. On the other hand, some of them could be collectors' items.

It is quite interesting to note how writing styles have changed over the years. Early in the last century, people who were probably on quite intimate terms would correspond in a most formal style. 'My dear Miss Agnes Appleton . . . .' 'with kind regards, your affectionate cousin Cuthbert.' And the messages conveyed by the humble postcard were sometimes really quite vital and indicated a tremendous trust in the postal service to deliver. 'Tell John to pick me up at the railway station on Friday at 3 o'clock,' Elizabeth. Did John get that message? Is Elizabeth still waiting at the station?

I often have a thumb through the section depicting my own hometown of Preston in Lancashire; it's amazing what you can discover. I came across one featuring a photograph of some schoolchildren in costume creating an historical scene from the Preston Guild of 1922. It turned out that one of the young pages in the foreground was my mother now in her nineties. She was quite pleased to see herself although it was, as she pointed out, only the back of her head.

THIS IS THE LIFE, NOTHING TO DO, AND ALL DAY TO DO IT IN !

Typical English saucy seaside post card.

On a visit to one of these fairs in Cumbria with my wife we purchased a few cards although we're not really collectors. They depicted scenes of local interest from yesteryear. One of them was a view of the site where we have our caravan near Grange-over-Sands. It transpired that the old caravan in the photograph had been built by the current site owner's father and the message on the back written by her mother. Another one which we have on display in the caravan is from 1907. It shows a scene of Lake Windermere in a storm and the penciled message on the back by an optimistic visitor from Blackburn simply reads - 'We are doing Champion. Weather Grand.'

Isn't that just brilliant. You can almost detect the correspondent's Blackburn dialect. Far more colourful than 'Wish you were here'.

Preston Bus Station - from Britain's most boring postcard collection.

If you choose to venture 'off road' – you do risk venturing 'off bike'.

Pedalling along the High Street.

I kept telling a friend, about a mountain bike ride I'd experienced in the Lakes some twenty years previously. Twenty years must be the period in time that one's memory regarding pain and discomfort gives way to the recollection of joys and benefits.

Having persuaded him with my eulogy about the majestic views and the possibility of spotting a golden eagle and jet black, wild fell ponies, he agreed that it would be worth re-doing. A couple of weeks later we set off on the very same route I'd discovered in a little book on mountain bike rides. It started up from Hartsop in Patterdale to the Hayeswater Reservoir, then up to the overlooking hill called The Knott and eventually meeting the old Roman track along High Street.

I had warned my friend that he may have to carry his bike up some steep sections, this turned out to be an understatement as we walked alongside our bikes virtually all the way to the reservoir. Then it was a case of shouldering our bikes and plodding upwards for some two thousand feet to High Street. Now I'm in my mid-seventies, this new sport of 'bike-packing' doesn't get any easier, but thankfully my Marin mountain bike I'd picked up on a car boot near Milnthorpe for just £35 is really quite light, and a bit of foam I'd attached to the cross-bar did afford a bit of comfort for my own ancient frame.

I've been up to High Street fell waking on numerous occasions, always scanning the skies for that elusive golden eagle without success. Others are luckier, my daughter drove up to the head of Hawes Water a few years ago and didn't even have to visit the eagle-watch hide in Riggindale. As she got out of her car there was the golden eagle soaring above her.

Part of the flat summit along High Street is also marked on the map as Racecourse Hill. Some two hundred years ago this was the venue for a fair with horse racing, wrestling and other sporting activities. Barrels of beer were carted up for the event. Having wrestled our bikes up there we felt we had paid homage to those hardy souls from yesteryear.

The best part of our ride then lay before us. There's no real evidence of a Roman road other than a track and the documented knowledge of its existence. It was originally a high level route avoiding the dangerous forested areas below and possible ambush, linking the fort at Ambleside (Galava) with the one at Brougham (Brocavum). It goes on for easy pedalling mile after mile with majestic views across the roof of Lakeland to a point almost adjacent to the head of Ullswater where you leave the ancient Roman track and turn down towards the lake.

This stretch is a delight for any cyclist, you can virtually free-wheel all the way down to near Howtown on a pleasant track bordered with bracken, heather with a view of the lake and the surrounding hills. Delightful as it is, I did manage to fall off my bike going through the smallest of streams when my front wheel came to a dead stop against a boulder and I continued over the handlebars. No harm done though, I think my mini rucksack saved me from any serious impact. You have to expect that if you choose to venture 'off-road' – you do risk venturing 'off-bike'.

Eventually we reached Howtown, which is where I should have changed my route. The one we followed was the one whose difficulties my memory had failed to recall. It goes around Hallin Fell down to Sandwick by road and then follows a bridle track all the way to the southern end of the lake. This makes for an interesting walk with great views of the lake and no real problems for a fell walker, but it's not one I would even consider taking a horse down. It's a fairly rocky, up and down affair with no respite. Pretty scary I would imagine for both horse and rider. I'm told that 'real' mountain bikers can negotiate it, but I'm not convinced. The only saving grace for us, apart from the views, was a newly created little café converted from an old barn.

What we should have done, was to take the ferry from Howtown, back down the lake (at my age one has to consider survival) or to simply have taken the road around the top of the lake through Pooley Bridge and back along the far side of the lake. Several more miles longer, but a pleasant ride.

Possibly – maybe – next time?

Oh, to be beside the screeside.

I had a call from a chap at the Westmorland Gazette regarding a photograph I'd submitted some years ago for a competition. The twelve winning entries (which didn't include mine) were featured in their Lakeland calendar. He told me they were preparing a magazine feature of readers' Lakeland photographs and they'd come across my original entry in their photo files.

Photographic competitions always used to be the preserve of camera buffs and his questions did seem to be a legacy from that time. Back then, captions to photos were laced with 'camera speak' – lens types, shutter speeds, f-stops, apertures and the like. I had to admit to him that my little camera was an automatic, simple, compact, 'point and shoot' affair. Any expertise was simply in the direction I pointed it. These days, excellent photos can even be taken on your phone.

The photograph in question was taken from near the head of Wastwater, looking up towards the rugged heights of Scafell. In the foreground freshly mown hay was laid in two-tone green stripes curving around the contours of a steep field. It created an interesting pattern but also illustrated how every inch of available land in Lakeland is cultivated where possible.

His phone call did remind me of the day when I was there. It was following a long walk I'd planned along the top of the fells above the Wastwater screes, then negotiating a seldom-visited path at the base of the screes themselves. The Wastwater screes are probably one of Lakelands most iconic views, they never fail to impress. They appear to hang like grey curtains draped as a backcloth, falling directly into the cold, dark waters of the lake, the deepest of all Lakeland's lakes.

My walk started at the head of the lake and I made my way up to the trail along the fell top. The view from here is best described as being similar to a walk along Beachy Head. The land falls away dramatically and you are presented with a landscape far below, which takes on a pale, hazy hue and merges with the sea and sky over to the coast towards Sellafield. It's like looking at two distinct landscapes butted together along a torn line.

Whilst you imagine this view, I'll relate another photo story resulting from the same day. About mid-distance in this scene there was a patch of greener grass protruding out from the heights with a rocky cliff edge which dropped down to the screes and the lake below. I took a photo of this panorama and popped it on Photoshop when I got home. Right in the centre of the green I dropped a little white vertical line, about a quarter of an inch long and just one pixel thick with a little flag on top. I then posted this on to the 'blog' pages of a friend's website. She has a company which manufactures golf trolleys and apart from posting my cartoons, invites her customers to post photos of exotic golf courses from their travels. I captioned my little creation as Lakeland's most extreme Green at the Wastwater Golf Club. Some time later I received an email from a golfer who had risen to my fictitious challenge. Failing to find the Club on Google he'd contacted my friend with the website. Thankfully, he was quite amused to discover it was a hoax photo and his email congratulated me on my (single line) Photoshop expertise.

The path along the edge has the occasional break where you can peer down steep gullies to the lake below. I'm not really in the business of writing walking guides but I should point out that these gullies should not be entered. Even Alfred Wainwright didn't venture into their crumbling depths. There is a safe, natural descent at the southern end through a winding, bracken-lined path, down to a track by the River Irt and leading directly to the pathway along the base of the screes.

It's from here you start your real mini adventure. For the most part, the scree path is quite distinct but occasionally the stones become boulders and there are a couple of sections where the boulders are the size of armchairs.

Centuries of walkers have made little impression on these and the pathway becomes non-existent. You simply have to pick your way across till you find the path again. This is just a few feet above the waterline and can just about be spotted from the far shore. Looking through binoculars you can occasionally see walkers slowly edging their way along. There isn't any real danger of falling into the lake – but care should be taken on the rocks in case you turn your ankle. It's a long hop back to the head of the lake – a fairway too, if you're searching for a Golf Club!

WATERSTONES

5 ITEMS
OR FEWER

Waterhouse

Penyghent. The first of the three peaks challenge.

Note. *This little piece was originally written for the magazine* Lancashire and the Lake District Life. *I claimed this lovely area of Yorkshire just for the day.*

The Three Lancashire? Peaks.

Although I realize that this magazine is devoted to the wonders of Lancashire and Cumbria I'm going to write about the classic Three Peaks walk of Penyghent, Werneside and Ingleborough, normally referred to as 'Yorkshire's Three Peaks'.

Being born in Preston and raised in Penwortham I have the River Ribble in my DNA. So, a walk in Ribblesdale, visiting Ribblehead and circumnavigating the Ribblehead viaduct is simply exploring my Ribble roots. Besides, I can recall when both Coniston and Windermere were part of

Lancashire till someone moved the County borders. So, I will move this border myself – just for the day, and for the sake of this little piece, declare Ribblesdale as part of <u>my</u> Lancashire.

My fell walking friend and I thought we'd do a reconnaissance trip up from Horton up Penyghent, then across to Ingleborough and back.

The walk up Penyghent is short, only about two and a half miles from the car park to the summit. Then the long walk f to the distant Ingleborough is across limestone country, home to those who venture into the subterranean world of the potholes and spectacular caverns. It's not really my cup of tea, squeezing under claustrophobia inducing gaps, but I can quite understand its fascination to others, its cave systems can be linked for mile upon mile.

When I first started work in a Manchester studio, one of my colleagues was well into the activity, being a member of a speleological club. He would spend most weekends underground. One Monday morning Charlie didn't turn up. He'd been trapped underground by rising water levels. Charlie and chums were featured in the newspapers being feared lost but they returned from the

dead on the Tuesday. He told me that the passage they had used to enter a chamber had filled with water and they had sat on a ledge as the water rose up to their legs –

then gradually subsided to leave their escape passage free again. They emerged from the depths after three days underground to the applause of the rescue teams and the media.

Sorry, I digress from my visit to the summit of Ingleborough where we came across a party of junior school children from Bradford who were then on their last leg of completing the Three Peaks walk. A wonderful achievement for both them and their teachers. If a party as young as this had completed it, we would have no excuse.

We decided that for our attempt we would choose a rain free day. It didn't turn out that way of course. Having soon made our way up Penyghent, the long stretch to Ribblehead was quite easy going – almost down hill all the way. Stopping for a cup of tea at Ribblehead we took in the close up view of the magnificent viaduct whose arches stand over a hundred feet. This was the area where the River Ribble springs into life and starts its journey to the coast.

Crossing the rail line, it's was then a long slog over a drizzle covered Werneside which I shall dismiss from memory. Its only redeeming feature was a view as we descended from the clouds of the distant viaduct. Making our way across the valley we were then faced with a daunting stone stepped route up the steep side of Ingleborough. After such a long walk this was not a welcome sight but time was on our minds. To complete the walk in regulation time, if you are concerned with such criteria, it must be done in less than twelve hours. As it transpired, we completed it in a rather leisurely eleven hours.

Another friend's daughter and her family did the same walk a few weeks later with a fund raising charity organization. They split you up into little groups, each group with a guide. In their group they had a young woman who although having a big heart, unfortunately also had a figure to match. She was sporting a helium filled balloon featuring the logo of her chosen charity. Now, I don't really want to decry her efforts, she obviously meant well, but was obviously unprepared for the ambitious task despite the advice given on her entry literature.

The furthest she had previously walked was probably to the local cake shop. By the time they were reaching the base of Penyghent she was already languishing behind. Their guide, recognizing that this whole venture was beyond her capabilities, told the group to carry on and escorted the young lady back to Horton. He rejoined them later at the summit.

If you fancy doing such a walk, take along a little flag with a red rose on it. Stand on top of Penyghent and declare ownership of it for the County of Lancashire. Just for the day of course.

I'd let Yorkshire keep Werneside.

Treasure hunting.

Most weekends throughout Lancashire and Cumbria there are numerous car boots and tabletop sales, ideal hunting grounds for treasure seekers. Mind you, it's buried, you have to trawl through an awful lot of junk to find that elusive treasure, and you need to know what you are looking for. To that end our bookshelves have accumulated rows of books on all manner of collectables from ceramics to furniture. These days there are daily TV schedules full of programmes devoted to clueing viewers up to the value of their heirlooms, yet I could give you dozens of examples of folk selling items completely oblivious to their real value. Eager eBay vultures like myself, will swoop down and have them offered on line in a trice.

One of the programmes from the genre is called Flog-it. Not the sort of title one would expect from BBC2 but it's a sign of the times. Flog-it broadcasts from various venues around the country inviting viewers to bring along interesting items to be valued – and then to possibly be sold at auction. As they were visiting a school in Windermere near our caravan, we went along armed with a jardinière we had purchased in Southport back in the 60s. It had served its time in various locations around the house, survived the proximity of two children, seen off an aspidistra and eventually found itself relegated to the garage. It had been earmarked for eBay but was chosen to audition for television stardom.

We'd originally bought it purely because it was attractively designed in the Art Nouveau style and it was only years later that we gleaned from one of our books, it had been designed by Frederick Rhead, the father of Charlotte Rhead who became one of Britain's foremost ceramic designers. It was quite possible that the tube lined design motifs could have been created by Charlotte herself (further info from one of our books).

The Flog-it crew were quite impressed with our budding star. They filmed us as we endeavoured to appear knowledgeable whilst our jardinière strutted its stuff. As guardians we were invited to take our protégé along to the next stage in it's television career – the auction in Penrith. How would it fare? Would our ceramic starlet crack under the hammer?

Apart from eBay, my experiences of auctions are pretty limited. Not really a place to pick up a bargain unless you are very lucky. Good venues for sellers though. These days auction houses publish their catalogues on the Internet. Serious buyers can view the items from their armchairs and even bid over the phone.

All the items are displayed for pre-viewing and I have to say I wasn't impressed. It all looks like a pile of junk, which you would expect to be going for a song – but it doesn't. Everything sells, and for good money too. Our jardinière, with a reserve of £90, sailed away for £400. I don't think I would have achieved that on eBay. Another successful seller on the programme was a chap from Bolton who had discovered a piece of Whitefriars glass in a skip, which sold for £200.

With jardinière bound for aspidistras new and ourselves quids in, it was an entertaining day out with a good result. Quite an experience too, a thoroughly professional team making sure everything ran like clockwork.
As efficient as eBay I would say, and I think IBM runs that with millions of transactions daily where you can buy or sell anything. Just browsing on eBay can be entertaining. For example – let's just type in g, l, o, b, e – we instantly discover there are 118 globes for sale in the UK.

All this eBay activity is very sad I admit, I really am addicted. I'd better click off eBay's globes and try a real globe with Google Earth. This really is a fantastic web site, and it's free! You can enjoy a high definition, view of anywhere in the word. With Google Earth you can take control of the camera and move around your selected target (I think it's probably military sponsored technology). I've even floated above the little villages in Cyprus where my wife's parents came from. One of these is in Northern Cyprus where access was limited – but not to Google Earth, so I was able to fly unrestricted up into the Kyrenia Mountains.

What's all this got to do with treasure hunting? Well,

hovering about over the Fylde countryside I've spotted the outline of an ancient buried site only visible from above. Sorry, I can't reveal its location – I'm off on a treasure hunt. Next time my friends recognise me on Flog-it, I may be trying to flog a bronze-age helmet or a gold amulet.

Waterhouse

A damp course through the Crinkles

I set out bright and early for the fells. Well, early anyway, if not exactly bright. The forecast warned of wind and rain - but they can get it wrong can't they? I'd been planning a walk across the Crinkle Crags and had decided that this was as good a day as any. It wasn't.

Weather-wise it was a big mistake; it was definitely not a good day. Normally, better judgment prevails and I don't bother to venture on the high fells when the weather is bad. There are two basic reasons: a) because it is dangerous, and b) because it is pointless. So off I went regardless on my dangerous, pointless journey.

The Crinkle Crags (Old Norse for circle) are a series of five smallish (2816 ft) rugged peaks running like knuckles across the head of the Langdale valley. There are umpteen ways to approach them but I settled for the most obvious route via the valley itself.
This was one of my first walks since returning to Lakeland and I was armed with a glossy new guidebook to consult on route and a splendid new map.

The head of Langdale is dissected by a huge natural ramp of a hill called the Band which divides the valley into two lesser ones. Mickleden, overlooked by the impressive Langdale Pikes, and Oxendale, whose little beck I would follow before turning to climb steeply up besides a deep ravine. The Crags ahead were lost in low cloud but looking back the Langdale Pikes were still in view. There was still a chance the cloud would clear. Optimism is a wonderful virtue but must be the cause of many a disaster (this is a pessimistic view of optimism). So onward and upward.

By this time I had relieved my rucksack of various waterproof garments. I use the term 'waterproof' only because this is how they were labeled. The fact that they are not actually waterproof seems to have escaped the manufacturer's notice. The weather was not improving, it was also becoming quite windy and I was glad that I had my lumberjack style hat with sides that pulled down over my ears. It also had a peak, which is ideal for anyone wearing glasses in the rain. Rain generally converts glasses into bathroom windows but the peak serves you well if you trudge along with head lowered. At least you can see your feet and where to put them clearly.

Reaching the top of this first section I was well into the cloud. The area ahead leveled off and is the location of the attractively named Red Tarn. Lakeland has many high tarns, some dark and moody, some as attractive as you could ever imagine. Others such as Red Tarn fall into the 'dull pond' category. Granted my first impression was probably tainted by the day and the weather. Others will tell you it is a delightful tranquil pool set against a dramatic backdrop - but I've been there several times since and to me it's still a pond.

The path from here bears right and upward toward the first of the Crinkle Crags. I met the first of only a handful of pointless journey makers I would encounter. I nodded my wet head to a chap with his dog who emerged from the cloud above, then disappeared into the cloud below.

My guidebook had warned me of an obstruction in the pathway ahead ominously called the Bad Step. This, I was informed was a ten foot scramble up a rock face which shouldn't pose any real problems to the average climber although it was in an exposed precipitous area. There was however an avoiding route for those who couldn't manage it. A ten-foot wall of rock I reckon I could handle but being a bit of a whimp, exposed precipitous areas are not my idea of a day out. As a rule of thumb, I don't mind risking a tumble. Any fall that is the start of an event that doesn't stop, then I'm not too keen. As it turned out I lost the path at this point and I never encountered the Bad Step. In some ways this was a bit of a disappointment but at this stage I was already beginning to doubt the wisdom of the venture anyway. (Having returned to the area several times since, I can report that the Bad Step isn't so bad whichever way you approach it).

The elusive path came and went as I fumbled my way from crag to crag. Each of the crags has a steep rocky buttress facing Langdale, so naturally my route when not in touch with the path, tended to veer to the other side. The crags rise and fall quite steeply, each one offering the visitor incredible views on a good day and incredible danger on a bad one. In some ways my lack of visibility was fortuitous. Had I seen some of the dangers or potential disaster areas around me I may have well panicked. As it was I merely saw the dark shapes of the crags in front of me disappearing into the gloom, and descending I was preoccupied with keeping my feet on the rocky terrain. The actual views from the crags (when You have one that is) are most impressive with Scafell Pike (England's highest peak) immediately behind you.
I was on about the third crag that I met more pointless

walkers. A group this time, and as I approached I heard one of them remark to a friend, " Look, that chaps doing it without a map."   A map! What good would this do anyone in this situation? The furthest you could see was 10 yards. "Are these the Crinkle Crags?" one of them queried. "I hope so, " was about all I could offer, amazed that anyone could be in such a predicament. I mean, I knew I couldn't find the path half of the time, but at least I knew where I was. Well, almost.

Eventually, I calculated that following the fifth crag I should be at a point called the Three Tarns (three more ponds) from where a track would lead down The Band to safety. And so it turned out. Now that the danger was behind me I could sit for a while and enjoy my lunch. Finding a sheltered spot behind some large boulders, away from the driving wind, I tucked into a sandwich and a drink from my flask. At the time I figured that if anyone develops a flask that doesn't convert coffee or tea into some strange, bitter, lukewarm pond water they'd be on to a winner. (I've since discovered one that works) We only used to use them because we got to a stage when anything was drinkable.

I couldn't face the rest of my sandwiches. I didn't have a view or a comfortable seat, so packing everything away, I set off down The Band. Normally, after visiting a peak, I think the average fell walker feels rather pleased, a sense of elation, away from the world's problems and all that stuff - apart from having enjoyed the sheer majesty of the views. This time it was more with a sense of relief, though I did feel rather chuffed that my sense of direction and rather vague navigation technique had come up trumps. I wouldn't like to put this to the test on a longer journey.

Coming up The Band were three walkers, obviously bent on a similar pointless exercise. "Have you just passed the Three Tarns?" inquired the first walker. "I think I must have done," I replied feebly," I didn't actually see anything." At this point the three walkers should have decided that their pointless venture was indeed a pointless venture, but optimism rules. Onward and upward.

Part way down I was caught by the last walker I would see on my journey. He'd abandoned his walk after reaching the Three Tarns and good sense had put him in reverse mode. He was actually engaged on some navigation exercise for some youth leadership scheme or other, but had decided that today was not a good day on the grounds that you couldn't see. Well, some kids will at least be safe with him I thought, he certainly had more sense than I had.

By this time I was feeling rather damp. In fact I was feeling wet. I wasn't cold but I was wet. The 'waterproof' outer layer was at least acting as a wind barrier, but inside I could feel my clothes sticking to me. I was even wet inside my boots. Eventually I reached the Old Dungeon Gill Hotel and went straight into the Hiker's Bar. Now this is a civilized idea. The Hiker's Bar caters obviously for hikers. Wet hikers, muddy hikers, knackered hikers, whatever. The stone floor must have welcomed a million bedraggled dripping hikers over the years and the old church pew seating comforted a million weary bottoms.

I reached into my rucksack and even that was wet. I've discovered since that the rainwater had collected in the open bottle pockets at the sides and then seeped through the seems. My nice new guidebook and map was becoming a papier-mâché item by a process of osmosis and continued vibration. My remaining sandwiches were a sad, waterlogged heap. Next time I buy a 'waterproof ' garment I figured I would to test it in the shower. I needed a new waterproof rucksack too. It's an expensive business all this walking about.

A classic case of nostalgia

What criterion is used to determine how a motor vehicle achieves 'classic' status is difficult to define. It could be the total design concept, the sculptured flow of its lines or some feature of its engineering. Every decade throws up some obvious candidates and the motoring Oscars take their place in the motor show of fame.

These days, nostalgia seems to play more of a role in the nomination procedure. Any car to survive (by some miracle) from the 50s or 60s appears to have the 'classic' title tagged on. Motoring through these decades was certainly an exciting adventure. It was a period of boom and fairly full employment.
Britain had a motor industry it actually owned itself – and what a range of makes and models it boasted. Austin, Hillman, Sunbeam, Wolsley, Riley, Humber, Standard, Triumph, Rover MG, Jaguar, there must have been about twenty different marques. The man in the street was now able to drive in it – not just peddle down it. Mass motoring had arrived.

Occasionally you will see a survivor from this era advertised. Maybe it had been locked away, unused for decades or lovingly cared for by some enthusiast or simply rebuilt. It will be described in terms that its original glossy brochure couldn't match, and it's always a 'classic'.

Hillman California, mint, one owner from new – a 'classic'. Riley Pathfinder, a rare example of this 'classic' car. The 'classic' Humber Super Snipe. Triumphs 'classic' Roadster. Vauxhall Cresta, Standard Vanguard, Wolsley Hornet, Jowett Javelin, 'classics' all.

Instantly I'm taken back to those heady days when these new models were unveiled at the Earle's Court Motor Show and for reasons of nostalgia or whatever, I'm tempted. On one occasion a real rose
– tinted attack of nostalgia got the better of me and I went for a test drive in an MGB. I was in the grip of that same passion I held for it all those years ago. That throaty rumble of its exhaust, that short, stubby gear lever, an alloy and wood steering wheel. Never mind that the average current diesel hatch back could see it off.

The MGB of course was yet another 'classic' though in this case with some justification. It did however reveal a few bubbles of lurking rust in the usual vulnerable areas. My rose-tinted vision slowly began to merge to rusty orange and I declined from making an offer.

I've no doubt, if you're old enough, that as you read this you are recalling some car you, or your family used to drive back then. That really WAS a 'classic' wasn't it? Well, chances are, despite its sumptuous leather seats and opulent walnut dashboard, it was no such thing. More than likely it was just another overweight, temperamental, downright unreliable, badly designed box of rust.

What the average man in the street bought with his newly offered 'HP', his hire purchase easy terms, was in the main, a very average car. Most of them came equipped with a starting handle. A sort of built-in unreliability factor. This was an age when 'planned obsolescence' came with a vengeance into the marketing strategy. This manifested itself by way of a unique virulent strain of accelerated rust. I'm convinced that this escaped in the early 50s from some secret MOD laboratory, probably ate its way to freedom or was deliberately released by the motor industry itself. This MOD escapee could munch its way through a Vauxhall Victor in under a year and the beautiful, genuine classic, E Type Jaguar was one of its favourite snacks.

And what did the British motoring industry do about this? Nothing, naturally. If a car falls to bits – you sell another. Besides, even if the body was being chewed up from without, the engine was sure to finish the job from within. This 'classic' motoring age was a time when engines were past their peak at 80,000 miles and a new (reconditioned) engine was an oft-used option. Exhaust systems became exhausted themselves in a life span you could measure in months.

Many of these 'classic' motors were pretty basic. I can remember once showing off my new, non-standard chrome plated wing mirror. On another vehicle I fitted the latest in high technology, a pair of flashing indicators. Or was the real High Tech masterpiece, that bright orange, translucent plastic bug deflector perched on the front of the bonnet?

It's true, I was never at the luxury end of the car market, but even there, not many cars were fitted with a radio as standard. And if you did have one, did it always work? If you, or some other motorist in the vicinity didn't have some device called a suppressor fitted, then you were treated to a clicking stereo interpretation of your engine through your simple mono speaker. Heating systems (if you had the deLuxe model) in these 'classic' cars was even less than basic. Whilst hypothermia crept through your body, your feet were baked at the equivalent of gas Mark 7. The uncontrollable heating control had two basic settings, on, or off. On long winter journeys it could decide to be off, regardless of the setting.

Long journeys were more of an expedition. Driving down to London from my home in Lancashire, pre motorway for the most part, was quite a long-winded event. It was undertaken with crossed fingers and a fully paid up AA membership.

Don't misunderstand me. I'm as nostalgic for the period as anyone who lived for it. I recall the roads being less congested and petrol was only about three shillings a gallon (15p) – but the cars were – crap. Even the cars that Britain created that did deserve the 'classic' accolade were riddled with rust. As for the rest, well it took the Japanese to spell it out for us. We gave a whole industry away.

Perhaps I should simply overlook all these faults and endorse the 'classic' perception of these cars by investment and recoup some of the money I have lost over my motoring years. And I've certainly lost some. Worse still, I've let some slip away. As a student in the 50s I sold a 1932

Austin 7 with red leather bucket seats to a fellow student for £10. Now that was a 'classic' car.

Or was that just a 'classic' mistake?

Planning to go panning.

Thar's gold in them thar fells.

When I was a schoolboy I can recall the National Coal Board offered 'careers' in coal mining. It occurred to me, even as a young teenager, that this proposition had at least one basic flaw. As the sun came up, you would disappear down a hole in the ground – then emerge again just before sunset. Miners would also emerge looking like a troop of Al Jolson tribute acts, covered in coal dust and no doubt having lungs full of the stuff. How those Welsh miners managed to create such remarkable singing in their male voice choirs is a mystery. I would have thought they would have had to cough their way through every song.

Apart from that, although, mining disasters were not commonplace, they did occur. You never heard of office workers being trapped in a building if the ceiling had collapsed in the boardroom cutting off their only means of escape. As it was, I had other plans anyway, but there were areas in Lancashire and Lakeland where mining was the only real option. Sons had followed fathers down into that subterranean world for decades. Whole close-knit communities were founded on it and were destroyed when coal was no longer king.

Amongst my collection of books on Lakeland I have a couple on mining in the region. It's not that I have any intention of exploring old mine shafts. That prospect (if you pardon the pun) fills me with dread. I did once venture down a pothole as a Boy Scout and that cold, dark, very wet world I found was not for me. It was an adventure but not one I was eager to pursue, and certainly not one I would consider as a career choice. My interest in mining is purely to increase my knowledge of an area close to my heart. It's just learning what makes the place tick, as they say.

Mining in Lakeland goes back to before Roman times. It's hard to imagine a harder way to earn a living. Some of those early miners worked by candle light, deep in the depths of a mountain, chipping away at solid rock with the mountain itself trying to exchange its treasure for their lives. Hundreds must have perished down those shafts either buried or drowned – some never even to make it back to the surface.

Amongst the varied minerals man has extracted from these hills are iron, copper, baryte, lead, graphite, tungsten, clay, zinc and silver. There's only a passing reference to gold, but it is there. Probably because it has not yet been discovered in sufficient quantities to be mined commercially. In fact one elderly chap has been panning for gold for over forty years. Not that he has found much – but that's not the point. Perhaps he's not much good at it, or possibly he's been panning in the wrong location. He has found gold though and my theory is, that if he's found gold, then the forces of nature that produced it must have created more.

Actually, you don't need to rely on my theory because gold has been discovered in Mungrisdale, Dunmail Rise, Troutbeck and even over as far as Sedburgh. Possibly there are other areas where a small band of prospectors have discovered gold – but it would hardly be surprising if they didn't tell the world.

My first step is to buy a large, shallow wok, that should do the trick. I've seen the technique demonstrated on YouTube , it doesn't look that difficult. All I then need is a bit of luck. Don't get the idea that I'm expecting to find a retirement-sized nugget or to start a Klondike gold rush. Enough to make a ring would be great – or even enough to pay for my wok would be nice. Forget all that gold rush stuff. My idea of prospecting is sitting by a Lakeland stream in the sunshine on a camping stool. I'll be simply swilling gravel in my wok, listening to the radio and enjoying the view with a glass of stream-cooled beer and a miner's pasty. If I don't strike it rich it won't matter – my gold rush will be more of a gold saunter.

The best thing is, I won't be in the wrong place because nobody really knows where the right place is! It will be just like looking for a golden needle on Haystacks.

Captains log

I have never got down to mastering the fine art of water sailing. I did buy one many years ago – an old twelve foot national which was already well past its sail-by date when I acquired it. I took it out a few times and taught myself the basics but I had small children, played football and generally had other fish to fry.

It's something I always wanted to redress having spent over thirty years sailing sand yachts I still can't claim to be an all round sailor, so it was time to put things right. Besides, I figured with my experience it should be routine.

I came across a little Mirror Dinghy on eBay and managed to buy it at a ridiculously low price. It was a lovely little craft, completely refurbished, two sets of sails, a spinnaker (not that I knew what to do with it) and its own road trailer. I'd always wanted a Mirror since they first came on the scene in the 60s as a 'build it yourself' kit. Not that I ever fancied putting one together. With my ability to bodge, it would have been less than ship-shape. At the same time that I picked up my Mirror I received an invitation From The Oldie Magazine as a guest at the The Oldie of the Year lunch at Simpsons in the Strand. A lunch indeed to delay my launch.

The Oldie of the Year is a splendid affair sponsored by Swan Helenic. The guest list is one of those celebrity functions with a room bursting with names to drop, if you are so inclined – and me. Glancing round the room I spotted a chap in a rather smart Naval uniform. Must be a token sea captain representing the sponsors I figured, probably touting for passengers amongst the assembled celebs.

Eventually I got into conversation with a very pleasant lady who turned out to actually be just that. Lady West. Her husband was to be a recipient of one of the Oldie awards. Sir Alan West First Sea Lord of the Admiralty." Over here," she called, beckoning to my cruise line captain. He was a very pleasant fellow who chatted to me regardless of my Mr Nobody status and told me how he had been very lucky to delay his retirement in time to oversee the Bicentenary of the Battle of Trafalgar celebrations, the highlight of his Naval career. He mused on how he would occupy his newfound leisure time in retirement.

It occurred to me that here we were, both contemplating retirement from different ends of the gangplank of life. With my tongue firmly in my cheek I suggested that he should follow my example – and buy a Mirror Dinghy. I had this bizarre image in my mind of his local sailing club piping him aboard his dinghy, its red Mirror sails emblazoned with the gold stripes and loops of his Admirals rank. Fortunately he laughed before he continued his circulating – probably amongst guests with a more sensible level of conversation. So, my quest for sailing expertise had started at the very top. Chatting to the First Sea Lord. Now to launch my Mirror.

On my maiden voyage I nearly ended up as a sub-mariner as I accidentally kicked the self bailer off its sprung mounting and the water came flooding in as I made my way quickly to shore to fix it. I didn't keep the Mirror very long, nice as it was. As I intended to sail single handed for the most part, I found it a bit heavy and it was a bit of a handful for launching and landing. Besides I thought it would be a lot more convenient to buy a little plastic job with a self-supporting mast. Putting it back on eBay I made a substantial profit which allowed me to buy a much younger craft. It was a small dinghy made in the USA, virtually unbreakable, unsinkable and resistant to any kind of rot. All features that appealed to me. In truth it was really a junior sailors dinghy and a bit on the small side for me. The aluminium mast came in two sections and I did think they were a trifle on the heavy side for such a small craft.

Its maiden voyage was the lightest of light winds. Too light for my weight. Unless it was under way I had to sit, or kneel in the centre otherwise I would have it over. As I entered the southern end of Lake Windermere from the river, I was running down wind quite slowly and had just about reached the ferry embarkation jetty lined with people waiting for the ferry to arrive. I noticed a strange trundling noise emanating from my stern and glancing round I saw that my rudder wasn't fully down. To correct this I needed to give the tiller a sharp push so that the spring action would lock the rudder in position. The sharp push did the trick – but also tuned the rudder sharply, spinning the boat violently tipping it over in a second. The onlookers on the jetty must still be wondering how anyone could capsize a dinghy in virtually no wind. The mast, which I thought to be on the heavy side preceded to prove me correct and the whole outfit turned turtle.

My limited sailing experience has at least endowed me with the skills required right my craft and reaching up for the centre board, I put my full weight behind my effort to right her thinking that it would be quite a job to get her back from a completely upside down position. It just flipped over with ease – having parted company with the mast completely. Climbing aboard my oversized surfboard I realised that all was not lost. I could be reunited with my rig as it was still attached to the main sheet and I was able to haul it up from the murky depths of the lake.

Paddling across to the far shore I could imagine the laughter over on the far jetty. Resetting my sail I drifted back to my launch site. My enthusiasm dampened, my spirits sinking and my spectacles already sunk – probably now being worn by some pike.

The plastic dinghy was soon back on the market and realised another substantial profit. Perhaps I should forget about sailing and become a yacht broker. I seem to have a flair for that.

Global worrying.

An unpopular, fatalistic viewpoint. If you're at all conservation conscious, then you probably shouldn't read this. It's enough to make you hot under the collar.

Fossil fuels exist, man discovers that fossil fuels burn, man burns fossil fuels. It's as simple and as natural as that. The greenhouse effect is what inevitably will happen to a planet like earth. Global warming is just in the natural scheme of things.

Fossil fuels are there to be burnt. What else would you do with them? What's all the fossil fuss about? Every time you switch on the television we get another global warning, there's someone giving us grief about disappearing forests and climate change. The ice caps are melting, cows are farting tons of methane into the atmosphere, aerosols are time bombs, water levels are going up in the sea and down in the reservoirs. We're wasting our resources, polluting the seas, eating all the fish and choking the world with plastic - blah, blah, blah. It's becoming global boring.

I bet more people die from stress related illnesses, worrying about all this environmental catastrophe and holes in the ozone than they do from the resulting sun's radiation itself. And if the sun doesn't radiate you, some idiot will eventually throw a few nukes about in the name of religion and really do the job. Now there's something you could worry about. But climate change. That's the way of the world. It's what happens. Or global freezing!

A couple of decades ago we were told we were heading for another ice age. I bought some crampons and a sledge. Now it's not freezing –but warming up and we've all got to be concerned. I've got to worry about the fate of polar bears, any one of which would eat me soon as look at me.

What's bad news for our polar chums is good news for some other creatures. We'll have scorpions in Scunthorpe, and all manner of oversized creepy-crawlies. I bet the conservationists won't be jumping up and down to save the scorpion. They may well be jumping up though. The point is, if it's going to get warmer – it's nature's way. And Mother Nature will sort it out. She'll just move things about a bit and those that can't cope will join the Dodo.

Not only are we to worry about global warming, we've got to be concerned about how bloody green we are. I've always been green, long before I even knew I was – but now I'm supposed to worry about it. Green is a buzzword; it's a fashion thing. Now you've got to be anxious about how green your lifestyle is. Calculate your own carbon footprint. All I can say is, lighten up, get a grip – and just get on with your life. Buy a four by four if you must, the bigger the better, leave the gas on, burn coal if you want to, throw plastic in the landfill and even fly to work if you can afford it. Whatever you do, it won't make a spot of difference in the scheme of things. If you live on a flood plain, don't worry about it. Nothing's going to happen to you. It may affect your great grandchildren, but they will probably have more sense than to live on a flood plain. Millions of years ago the earth was struck by a giant meteorite – now that's what I call global warming, wiping out life on a grand scale. Volcanic eruptions are reputed to have done likewise. It will happen again, some day. Probably not for a thousand years or so, but it will happen. What of global warming then. Who will care about the effects of the preceding year's climate changes? And when it does – bingo, game over. Do you live near volcano? Are you expecting an asteroid delivery in your area? Are you worried about them? Of course not.

Eventually, we'll crawl out of the sea and begin our ridiculous yet wondrous evolutionary journey all over again. We'll create our civilisations and our religions with their subsequent wars, and science will help us to progress to the point where we are now – then some bright spark will raise the alarm. What about the global warming? - Or global freezing or whatever global malfunctions they come up with to worry about. Then guess what. Whumph. Another asteroid will pay us a call.

Global warming, I couldn't give a methane expulsion. Besides, I've got enough to worry about. Does the green bin collection come this coming Monday or the next? I've got loads of bottles, plastic and paper to put out.

watahouse

Lakeland's islands

An inverted view of Lakeland.

I think it's fair to admit that now I'm in my mid seventies, the term 'fair weather' could prefix any of my current outdoor activities. Cycling in the wind and rain was always about as enjoyable as a cold shower and these days, paddling my kayak into a stiff breeze comes under the general heading of 'why bother?' The days when I had the discipline to take me for a daily run regardless of conditions are gone. Granted, this afforded me a level of fitness I will never regain, and that smug feeling I felt as I bounded past someone half my age as they sheltered from the rain is unlikely to return.

This 'fair weather' rule particularly applies to fell walking and any walk is now planned with the weather forecast taking priority. Trudging along a Lakeland path through drizzle, or sitting on a wet slate slab eating a rain soaked sandwich is now a thing of the past. Dedicated fell walkers are welcome to this self-inflicted ritual – I'll come out to play and join you - when the sun does!

Having said all that, I did plan a winter walk up Coniston Old Man a few weeks ago with a friend, and even on the day before, the weather forecast promised warm air and low wind. When we set off before daybreak from near Preston it was in thick fog. Not really a problem as I figured when the sun did to turn up, it would burn this off by the time we'd reached Coniston. However, this didn't materialize and driving along the road at the side of the lake we only had fleeting glimpses of its still water, shrouded in a pale grey blanket.

Reaching the village, we turned sharp left and wended our way up to the Walna Scar road car park. The car park is just one of those that fell walkers 'in the know' have used for years to save themselves several hundred feet of tedious steep ascent. The National Trust has yet to plant a meter on it. The Walna Scar road from this point is really just a quarry track leading onto an ancient packhorse route over to Seathwaite.

As we drove up, I remarked, with more hope than conviction, that we would probably emerge onto the fell side with something more than our current two hundred yard view. Any real prospect of a rewarding walk up the fell though was looking doubtful. My friend opened the gate ahead and I drove through on to the fell side – straight into a completely different word, like entering Narnia, a world of blue sky and sunshine.

A couple of other cars were already there and we all took in the amazing unfolding view. The full impact of this was further realized with an increase in elevation. Lakeland, as far as the eye could see in any direction, was covered in a blanket of white cloud, with only the fells themselves visible above a milky white sea.

View from Coniston Old Man.

Apparently, (as Google tried to informed me) this phenomenon is caused by a temperature inversion, when a warm, air mass moves over a colder denser one, trapping any clouds below it. No doubt seasoned fell walkers may well have witnessed this remarkable effect several times – but this was a first for me. The full spectacular vista was seen even more clearly from the summit. Coniston Old Man is one of Lakelands highest peaks and commands views across Lakeland. The view south over to Morecambe Bay had taken on a futuristic view of a time when global warming had reached its terrifying conclusion. The sea and cloud had conspired to give this doomsday effect when the sea would have reclaimed vast areas of land. The Coniston valley and the lower fells had simply linked up with the Bay and the village of Coniston was lost like Mardale in its depths.

Normally you can identify various other peaks rising up across the landscape – but on this day they were each isolated like islands. Anyone who had ventured into the fells, regardless of their vantage point from Kentmere to Wasdale, would have enjoyed the same spectacular experience. It was a pity to have to descend from the summit, but although this remarkable effect was caused by a 'warmer' air mass – it was accompanied by an icy cold wind from which only the massive stone cairn offered any protection.

Over the years, I have had many memorable days out in Lakeland but this short walk has to rank amongst my favourites. A truly magical experience.

"Anything we say may be taken down and used in evidence."

"Wot's up wi thee? Thaz a fizzog like a line o' wet washin."

Quick as a snig.

'Tekin a sken' at a few Lancashire sayings .

I recall my late mother referring to anything that moved fast was *'quick as a snig'*. A snig being an elver, or young eel, which when confronted by an obstacle on its migratory path up stream, would take to the river bank and slither through the wet grass. Apparently, it was common practice way back in the day, to await the arrival of the unfortunate mass of squirming elvers and redirect their new destination into local frying pans.

There's a whole dictionary of Lancashire words, as with any county of course, and I could research these for a possible future little piece -but it's the phrases used that you can't help but raise a smile at. Most of these are long out of use, often referring to household chores, physical characteristics or situations that no longer exist. I had to enlist the help of a few older folk to recall some they remembered from their past.

Although I do have something of a Lancashire accent myself, with dropped 'h's and drawn vowels, writing in dialect is probably not my forte and I apologize to any purists out there. The problem with reading written dialect (as in poetry) is that you need to have an ear for the accent and an understanding of the local vocabulary. It's obviously written phonetically and I find it difficult to translate even with the benefit of my accent. If it is recited, then I can pick it up straight away.

The good old lavatory must be the source of many Lancashire sayings, though never referred to in full but often in its simple form of '*lavvy*' which is probably universal. Decorum dictates that one would never let you tell someone asking for your mother, that she was on the lavatory, but – '*She can't come to't door, she's on't doings*' would be an acceptable alternative. Both door and doings should really be spelled something like '*doower*' and '*dooin's*' but it all becomes like some written foreign language. Another word describing the *lavvy* is in the phrase – '*E's locked h'sen in't clodgie*'.

I love this this simple exclamation of hunger – '*Ah cud eyt a buttered frog*'. Or an old favourite – '*Mi belly thinks mi throat's bin cut*'. A buttered frog is about as appealing to me as a plate full of fried baby eels, but then, some folk eat snails and oysters. Perhaps my palate needs educating – I'll pass on that.

There are lots of derogatory remarks about individual's unfortunate looks or moods that often *hit the nail ont' th'ead*. Anyone sulking could well be described as - '*Tha'z a face like a line o' wet washin'*'. Some unfortunate soul not blessed with good looks could be referred to a having – '*A face like a melted wellie.'* Worse still, the fellow who had – *'A face like a farmer's bum on a frosty morning.'* Frankly, I don't think the state of the weather would make much difference to his obvious lack of appeal.

Why anyone would need to comment on the size of someone's teeth does sound a bit insensitive but - *'Ah bet tha cud eyt an apple thro a barbed wire fence,'* does illustrate the unfortunate recipients problem. Probably one he was well aware of himself.

Anyone failing to hit a given target could well be described by the expression – *'He cudn't 'it a cow's arse wi a banjo'.* Why a bovine backside was a target, or even why the weapon of choice was a banjo, remains a mystery. Someone, somewhere must have coined the phrase.

The word 'arse' crops up again when describing someone whose ability is in question – *'Tha'rt as useless as a one legged man at an arse kicking contest.'* I'm now in my seventy sixth year and up to now I've not yet encountered an arse-kicking contest (though I have heard of clog wearing, Lancashire shin kicking combatants) but I have to agree that it does add something extra to the heightened level of skill required by our amputee contestant. I don't think the Olympic Committee is ready yet for either of these Lancashire sports.

Another of my mother's expressions, probably referring to my own lack of action was – *'Standin' theer like cheese at fourpence'.* I never really understood where that phrase came from. Was fourpence expensive back in the day? Perhaps it needs updating to – *'Standing theer like cheese at four quid'.* *'Yer 'avin' me on a butty'* is a phrase meaning you're having me on and an idle person is *'Standin' theer like one o' Burton's dummies'*. There are many, which are still in use today – *'Tha meks a betta doower than a winda'* is obviously directed at someone obstructing your view. On the subject of *'doowers'* – *'Put wood int' th'ole on yer way out'*.

Ay up, mi spell check's feelin' badly.

Freight train, freight train . . .

. . . going so fast. Working at my desk with one ear listening to the Radio, I turned up the volume when I heard a familiar sound and the gentle voice of Nancy Whisky's skiffle classic filled my room and my head. Freight train, freight train, going so fast . . . I was a passenger on the main line to Nostalgiaville. I recalled that same 'freight train' song being driven along by six high-pitched schoolboy voices. The strumming of three novice guitarists punctuated at the point where a chord change was required with a hastily whispered instruction. T'chang - t'chang, "G7," t'chung - t'chung. Behind this rhythmic strumming, the beat was plucked from a tea chest base and a washboard chattered its percussive rhythm as thimble-clad fingers skittered across its corrugated aluminium surface. The melody rang out above the nervous guitars from a tuneful, confident banjo. Its player was also the source of the instructive chord change whispers. This was the 50s phenomenon of 'skiffle' at its rawest, and we were The Scratchers.

The name Scratchers was not derived from the action of the guitars or the subsequent sound created. Our talented banjo-playing leader had the surname Hitchen, pronounced locally as 'Itchin'. The ironic fact that he also suffered from eczema of the hands and fingers left his choice of nickname a mere formality. He was Scratch and we were the Scratchers.

The Scratchers were born in a scout hut in Penwortham in the early 50s but the name was soon changed, not to protect the sensitivities of our itchy fingered leader, but to give the band a more 'folky' sound and we became The Bunnock Ramblers. A name derived from an area of Lower Penwortham, where the story goes that a wagon loaded with barrels of treacle overturned on Pear Tree Brow and all the housewives rushed to scoop up the treacle to create 'bunnock cakes' (parkin).

My choice of tea chest player offered me the chance to pluck my way through any tune with no musical skills whatsoever and to pretend I was an accomplished exponent, adding variations to the base line with syncopated rhythms. The actual results were more that the base would be in pursuit of the rhythm instead of leading it. A stylized American freight train running round the four sides of my tea chest was a simple silhouette design with the name of the band in bold, spiky lettering. Had we made it to the top like our contemporaries the Beatles or the Stones, my tea chest would probably be on offer today at Christie's – but alas, not for it's artistic merit.

We did have our bookings though, and rambled our way round countless village and church halls in the Preston area, even performing for the Mayor at the Town Hall in Preston. I can still see the strained looks on the aged audience's faces as these strange boys created alien noises for their entertainment. We played in the now long gone Queens Theatre in Blackpool in a skiffle contest and a gig at the Marine Hall in Fleetwood. We even performed (uninvited) at Butlins in Filey.

It wasn't long after my trip down memory lane (or line) I received a surprise e-mail from a long lost Rambler. I hadn't seen or heard from him in nearly fifty years. His wife had spotted my name on the Internet and we arranged to meet up on the motorway, spending a pleasant lunch reminiscing on old times. He'd done quite well for himself having become a Captain of Industry and was now retired, we discussed the idea of a Ramblers' reunion.

Reunions enter your vocabulary any time after the age of sixty and I've been to one or two. You know the routine - everyone looks older than you think you do and you all promise to keep in touch but seldom do. Then you return home wondering what sort of impression you left.

Somehow, my long lost Rambling friend had cleverly persuaded me to organize the whole reunion event. I figure that the delegation of tasks is obviously how one becomes successful in business. Eventually I managed to trace all six Ramblers as none had rambled too far and were all based throughout the northern counties.

We all met for a weekend at a hotel in the Lakes along with our wives and the whole thing was a huge success. I suppose the difference being, that we were all good friends as lads as opposed to simply being work mates. We'd enjoyed each others company then and still felt the same today. The weekend was filled with a million memories of our rambles. Unfortunately tape recorders were not available to us at the time of our rambling and nothing remains of our efforts - this of course may be a blessing.

Freight train, freight train going so fast.   Like life itself.

"...and remember our slogan — 'A jolly Santa is an employed Santa'."

"There's just no call for animal acts these days."

Funny way to earn a crust.

Surviving as a cartoonist can be as frustrating as it can be rewarding. In my case it suited my lifestyle. Being a lazy fellow I would prefer to be on the golf course, the fells or on the beach rather than sat at my desk. This has resulted in never achieving a 'big name' status and consequently my rejection slips are numerous.

To be fair to the various editors, I often review my failed offerings and agree that the ideas my not be as amusing as my initial enthusiasm would have had me believe. Other times I get drawings returned that I still believe to be really funny (though I say so myself), I even have one on my wall rejected by the Oldie no less – which depicts a frustrated Jesus attempting to take a bath and only being able to walk on the water.

Actually getting your work to the various editors is a hit and miss operation in itself. I used to post stuff to Private Eye in the days when Richard Ingrams ran the show there. My cartoons would be returned with a slip saying 'Sorry – try Punch'. Amusing the first couple of times but it did become a bit irritating after a while. Later on when the Oldie came into being I was quite successful with my cartoons.

"The thing is Ivan, we're more of a traditional circus!"

Indeed, Mr Ingrams stated in the introduction of the first Oldie cartoon book how pleased he was to come across cartoonists who were completely new to him. Obviously our dear Editor was well protected at the Eye from new contributors.

My first drawings for the Reader's Digest followed a bit of self-promotion which nearly backfired. I submitted a few slides of my cartoons (long before the age of emails and Internet) and the art editor replied by letter stating that he liked my drawings but asked if I could reduce the size of my characters' noses. My response was an illustration of a chap with a bandaged nose and a note to say that my noses were not to be cut as they served as direction indicators.

Thankfully my frivolous reply was accepted in the spirit it was intended, and it resulted in a fifteen-year relationship with the magazine.

I've had work published in several leading magazines but my favourite was always Punch (even before the Eye suggested I should try it). My mother used to read Punch and it was always my
ambition to grace its pages since I was a small boy. Imagine my delight when the first cartoon I ever
submitted to them was accepted. The same cartoon

". . . perhaps a little light exercise?"
1970, my first drawing in Punch Magazine.

was also published in that year's 'Pick of Punch.' At that time I never became a Punch regular due in part to my lazy gene, though I did become one some years later when the magazine was resurrected by Al Fayed. Unfortunately it descended into a desperate rag towards the end and I'm proud to say I'd abandoned ship long before its eventual demise.

There are times as a cartoonist when everything goes to plan. Instead of sitting by an overflowing wastebasket amidst a pile of screwed up ideas, your drawings just fall off the pen and straight off to the post-box. I once had nine cartoons published in Punch in the same issue – and that was before it began its slide into oblivion (I don't think I was the cause). Other times, ideas are harder to come by, though my background in advertising was a real benefit. Creating ideas to a deadline is a pressure you learn to live with. Failure isn't an option.

Being what you could call a 'jobbing' cartoonist I have been exposed to the increasingly bizarre world of political correctness. This manifests itself in all manner of directives before you begin. I used to illustrate for a publisher who produced a series of books teaching English to foreign students. No female flesh was to be shown lest it should upset Moslem students and any suggestion of a cleavage could result in a fatwa. This never really cramped my style, as cleavages were never my forte and my cartoon women look far better clothed. Other diktats may state that any group of people must include an ethnic, gender and age mix. Local authorities are even worse for this PC nonsense and often require the inclusion of a token disabled person. I've even had a cartoon changed to substitute the female in the drawing to male because the situation made the female depicted (and therefore the whole sex) look silly. The alternative was apparently ok. Illustrating an ethnic mix can have its own problems. This has to be achieved without making the characters archetypical. No easy task for a cartoon which often relies on simplistic visual devices. In my cartoons the normal average bloke looks a bit strange to say the least – what chance has a Chinaman got. These days I could be accused of racism for making my cartoon look funny!

"It's a duvet."

Increasingly I turn work away knowing that it will be fraught with such restrictions. Previously I was offered a lot of this PC drivel via my ex agent and used to accept it on the grounds that it was very lucrative. Even with my agent taking 33%, the fee was still far higher than I would ever have had the nerve to command. I once did a two-hour cartoon of a van driven by Father Christmas, which my agent charged the client £1500. Sadly, such commissions were thin on the ground and the rest of the stuff I found quite unappealing. Only last week I did a drawing for a company which was to illustrate a seedy looking character printing his own money in a dingy cellar.

The comment came back from the client –'lose the cigarette'. Smoking today is obviously regarded as even further up the PC league table than forgery!

I think I'm becoming a grumpy old cartoonist. I stopped doing greetings cards because I was subjected to increasingly annoying requests. 'We like the idea but can you make the characters into furry animals', Apparently they sell better. I can't argue with sales figures, but I can say sorry, no thanks!

The old shambles, Lancaster Roas, Preston.

Edwin Beattie's recording studio.

As a youngster, often following a visit to the Cinema Club on Saturday mornings, I would pop into Preston's Harris Museum and Art Gallery. Hardly in the pursuit of culture, or to immerse myself in fine art, it was just a place we kids could run around, up and down the stairs and in and out the various galleries to the annoyance of the curators. There were of course some interesting exhibits that would grab the imagination of a small boy.

In 1970 (long after my boyhood) they put on display, the complete skeletal remains of a 13,500 year old, ice age elk, discovered in Poulton which has two barbed points embedded in it, this being the earliest proof of human occupation in Lancashire. Kids love this kind of thing.

Back then, I was always interested in (though never really understood) the Foucault pendulum which was a weighty metal ball hanging by a wire through the open circular central atrium for several floors, and its movement, activated by the earths rotation, created a reasonably accurate timepiece. No doubt this was often pushed out of kilter by mischievous fingers (not mine) to the annoyance of the frustrated curators. When my daughter was a young student teacher in London, she took a party of rowdy school kids to the Natural History Museum in Kensington. They were running riot around the place and one of the curators collared my daughter asking, 'Who's in charge of you lot?'

She soon learnt how to control children in her care. My mother was also a teacher and back in the 1920s her first post was at a one-roomed school somewhere behind the Parish Church in Preston. The day she arrived, the caretaker presented her with a cane. She told me, with that cane in hand, she never looked back. How times have changed.

What really caught my young eye in the Harris Museum, was not the high art of Stanley Spencer, which is one of the gallery's prized possessions but a series of water colours of Victorian Preston by Edwin Beattie. These were situated on the stairway and captured the town (not yet a City) as it had been for centuries, before the new buildings such as the Town Hall, dragged the town into the new industrial age.

We are in fact, indebted to the Preston Guardian Newspaper who commissioned Mr. Beattie to produce his body of work. He was gainfully employed by them for a good decade till about 1899 on this project.

Edwin Beattie was not a great artist, but he did have a passion for recording old buildings and streets in Preston, which he created with accurate, painstaking detail. Every shop sign or name was recorded. The cobbles, flagstones, sagging rooflines and chimney pots, all featured just as they were. His painting of the Lime Kilns on Aqueduct Street depicts workmen repairing the 100 ft. high chimney and roof. His illustration shows how the steeplejacks scaled the heights on incredibly long, simply lashed together, wooden ladders.

Edwin unfortunately also had a passion for ale and many of his paintings appear to have more ale than watercolour about them. On some of his paintings the perspective certainly does take on a rather ale induced slant. It has been said that often to settle a bar bill, or to supply a demand for his work, he would sometimes allow a friend to produce work in his name.

A few years ago I acquired an original Edwin Beattie painting from an auction at Salmesbury Hall. It is of the 'Shambles' on Lancaster Road. A row of ancient houses and shops, which were to be demolished to make way for the new building programme. Edwin painted this several times, originally from one of his brother's photographs. It was probably one of his favourite scenes and no doubt he could even paint it from memory. The one I acquired could be one of the first he created as it is dated 1879. I think that it was painted on one of his good days too because the slick confident brush strokes show no sign of his penchant for a tipple. I am quite proud to own this little piece of old Preston.

Edwin lived for a period on Fishergate, Preston, and quite possibly visited my great grandfather's shaving rooms just down the road. It's a pity he didn't create an unpaid account and settle it with a painting of the premises. This would be worth a few shillings these days. Back then, Edwin used to charge 7s 6d for each watercolour – or 13s6d if you wanted it framed.

His paintings of Preston surely deserve a permanent display somewhere, perhaps alongside photographs of the locations as they are today. It would be a wonderful legacy to the City.

"I'll try the filets de maquereaux au vin blanc
- with a large curried chips and mushy peas!"

The Royal Picardy, the grandest of grand hotels, sadly destroyed during WW2.

Bond Street by the Sea.

I was invited over to the rather chic little French town of Le Touquet, just down the coast from Boulogne, to a jumelage (twinning) celebration for char à voilistes (sand yachters). Le Touquet has a novel approach to twinning. They have the usual twin town arrangements, which, at the risk of appearing cynical, do seem to be jolly trips abroad for councilors at the rate payer's expense – but at Le Touquet they also twin organizations, choral societies, art groups, clubs devoted to various sporting activities and hobbies, that sort of thing.

My connection was with the Club de Char à Voile which was twinning with my own club and also with clubs from various other countries. I wasn't selected to attend as someone particularly special in the sport, I was the only person available that particular weekend and I'm also a friend of the chap who was running the club at Le Touquet. I'm not one to turn down a free weekend in France –

probably this taste for freebies shows I'm the right material for elected office and to become a councilor (well, perhaps not).

If there's one subject I can bore the pants off anyone with, it's sand yachting, so I will endevour to keep my references to the sport, short. I will however extol the virtues of this lovely little town. I'd quite happily retire there if I had enough euros. It's known as Le Touquet, Paris Plage – on account of it being the coastal retreat for many well-heeled Parisians. It has several chic little shops, restaurants and art galleries, two and a half golf courses, an airport and for the most part it is set in a pine forest which also hides some of the most exquisite (and expensive) homes you could imagine.

Whilst I was swanning around the Hotel de Ville, playing the part of a visiting dignitary, I was given a folder containing Le Touquet info. This included a potted history of the place which I found quite interesting and packed with facts and figures which enables me to do this little travelogue for you. Fortunately, this was in English as my French has hardly progressed since I left school (and it was pretty poor then).

For example, during the last war, Le Touquet was host to a very unwelcome body of 40.000 German troops waiting to invade Britain. A sort of planned D-day but in reverse. To make this invasion run efficiently, they decided to concrete the entire sea front. If you ever want anything concreting, give it to a German company, they have a talent for this kind of work there are examples of this all the way down to Normandy. This rather brutal landscaping project was however, completed with total disregard to planning applications which upset someone in Whitehall who are sticklers for planning approval. Subsequently allied bombers were dispatched to remove it with 2,000 bombs. The result of this is today's Le Touquet's sea front now has a very attractive modern holiday town look.

Going back to Le Touquet's beginnings, it didn't really take off as a resort until near the end of the 19th century, and prior to WW1 it had become the venue for the smart set from both London and Paris as it lay exactly mid way. It was 'continental' for the British yet paradoxically 'English' for the continentals. Le Touquet,-'Paris Plage' was also known as 'Bond Street –by-the-Sea'. It was once described by a French writer as a little piece of England washed up amongst the pine trees of Boulogne. The original pine forest planted by a Parisian lawyer, Mr. Doloz in 1864 to surround his chateau. The chateau later became the first of two casinos.

Baron Pierre de Coubertin, (founder of the revived Olympic Games) was appointed as director of sporting activities. A golf course was created along with a racecourse and all manner of events took place. They even had the latest 'flying machines' on the beach and char à voiles (you know what they are by now). One of those early aviators, Louis Bleriot was also a leading member of the char à voile set and the club there still boasts his name. This was a glorious period in Le Touquet's history with Europe's wealthy making it one of their playgrounds.

It became a hospital town during WW1 and apart from the British Army using the golf course for machine gun training (jolly bad form I'd say), it remained unscathed. For many of the unfortunate young men who didn't survive Le

Touquet's hospital care there's a military cemetery just across the River Conche at Etaples. Were told that it was re-named Eat Apples by the Canadians but I think if anyone could pronounce the name of a French town it would be the Canadians. Perhaps they simply got the blame for the Brits lack of linguistic ability.

Between the wars was Le Touquet's golden period. It was the haunt of the world's royalty, politicians, millionaires and film stars. Superb hotels befitting this clientele were built in the 20s along with a second casino. In 1927 the casino takings were the highest in France. Le Touquet had its own airfield, racecourse and the finest art deco swimming pool in Europe (now demolished). They even devised a bizarre golf match during an air show where competitors threw their golf balls on to the greens from aeroplanes. This was the forerunner of the jet set – the propeller set at play.

WW2 was a complete disaster for the town due to the afore mentioned German Troops. Whole areas were reduced to craters and rubble. The millionaire's playground became a minefield and the most heavily mined town in the whole of France. The departing German troops left a parting gift of some 75,000 mines set in every part of the town. Le Touquet's grandest of all grand hotels, the Royal Picardy, which probably housed the German High Command, had also been destroyed.

Le Touquet rebuilt itself after the war and once again catered for the rich and famous. Many celebrity figures had homes there and although the Royal Picardy no longer existed, The Westminster Hotel became the flagship. The Westminster does give you an idea of what Le Touquet style was all about. My wife and I were treated to a night there once. The floor to ceiling marbled luxurious bathroom was a splendid affair and the white bathrobes embroidered with the initials HW of the hotel were exactly the same as my wife's. No, we didn't take one home accidentally, but I have to admit, it crossed my mind.

There's a particularly interesting fish restaurant on the Rue Metz. It's one of those you may recall from your school French lessons, where Mr. Dupont selects his lobster from the tank at the front of the establishment. The décor is nothing to postcard home about, but it's worth a visit. They also sell large jars of that wonderful Bouillabaisse which I always used to bring home from my visits to Le Touquet till I discovered the same thing available in Tesco's. A sand yachting friend always insisted of returning home with some Camembert which got riper with every mile back to the north of England. I'd complain that it was available from any deli counter – and brought over in refrigerated transport. "Oh, it's not the same," he used to argue, and compounded our 'old sock' smelling journey by smoking his pipe.

I do have a little sorry tale about that pipe too. On another visit to France, an inebriated friend who'd over imbibed on the race sponsor, Ricard's free samples, took this pipe and to make some point regarding its unfortunate aroma, stuffed it with a piece of dried dog poo, then lit it, much to the annoyance of my friend. He then compounded this by dropping it and breaking the bowl. On returning home, our repentant reveller decided to replace the pipe and took it along to a pipe shop. The owner, sniffing at the bowl with some alarm, enquired what kind of tobacco he had been smoking. "Oh, just something I picked up in France," he replied.

I apologize for that little interruption to my travelogue. I'll return to the Rue Metz restaurant where I once dined with a group of German sand yachting friends who immediately took on the role of Mr. Dupont, perhaps they used the same French lesson books, and promptly depleted the lobster tank of its finest specimens. They then perused the wine list with no regard to costs. I selected something from lower down the menu with one eye on my wallet as I was also funding a young French student who was my co-pilot at the regatta we were all attending. At the end of the meal l'addition was then simply divided up equally and my humble choice perhaps becoming the most expensive monk fish since the days of the Royal Picardy – if they ever served such a lowly fish dish?

I used to harbour ideas about opening an English Tea Shop in Le Touquet. Not a Salon de Thé, but a real 'Tea at the Ritz' affair with English china crockery doilies, cream cakes, delicate sandwiches, radio four in the background and English newspapers on poles. I'd even have a picture of the Queen on the wall. It would be a real wow with the English and French alike.

When my granddaughter was doing her A level French, I thought it may help her if she spent some time in France with friends to look after her. Another friend who was the Director of Tourism for Le Touquet. He gave her a summer job in an information kiosk on the promenade. She spent most of her time there speaking English to English tourists, at least I know the clientele for my English Teashop is there in force.

There, I've given you a little taste of Le Touquet and hardly mentioned sand yachts The only thing for you now is to discover the place for yourself. If you do manage to get to Le Touquet, pop down to the Club de Char à Voile on the promenade, where you can hire a little mini char à voile and follow in the tyre tracks of Louis Bleriot.

Waterhouse

Bonkers. The decline of conkers.

For a game that has been recorded as being played possibly by yourself, your father, his father's father and so on back to 1821 and probably unrecorded back to Roman Britain or beyond, the humble game of conkers has been itself conquered.

Many youngsters these days may not even know what a conker is. They may know of course that it is the fruit of the horse chestnut tree, but not that it is the forbidden fruit, expelled from the schoolyard due to its life threatening dangers. You think I'm being over dramatic? Well listen to this -

Its decline began several decades ago by misplaced concerns about health and safety. It was banned in some schools initially by some headmasters worried about litigation should one of their charge sustain injury from a flailing conker. In fact there was probably more chance of this occurring from the conker collecting process. In my village, no conker tree within a two-mile radius was safe from being ravaged by hordes of junior harvesters armed with lengths of wood which were hurled into the branches to dislodge the conkers. These would return to earth like clubs onto the heads below. I will accept of course that many a tiny hand was rapped by an over enthusiastic, ill-aimed swing or that pain was often induced when the tangled strings would grip like a tourniquet.

I can't recall a single serious injury ever being recorded at the hands of a conker but a friend tells me that at least one youngster a week is taken to hospital from her son's school following a rugby tackle. Imagine the outcry if the health and safety brigade tried to ban rugby. One headmaster, sympathetic to the cause of the conker, hoped to allay such fears by organizing a Schools Conker Competition in which all competitors were issued with safety goggles to protect their eyes from conker shrapnel. Unfortunately, the idea backfired, as it was perceived by the health and safety vigilantes as a necessary requirement. No game of conkers could be played without them – otherwise blindness was a distinct possibility and added this to their list of dangers.

The final nail in the conker's coffin came when they came up with a bizarre story that the conker could cause anaphylactic shock to the growing number of kids with nut allergies. This, despite it being pointed out at the time, as not being possible (I told you it was claimed to be life threatening). The health a safety brigade however, won the day with their fabricated stories, claims and fears. The historic game being banned in all schools. No doubt they have now turned their vigilance to something equally innocuous.

So, today's kids now grow up in safety, apart from the dangers offered by almost everything from skateboards to skittles. They are unaware of the serious business of creating a hard conker. The secret alchemy techniques concerned with baking or soaking in vinegar. They will never know the joys of their conker gaining status through victory over other higher value conkers. A 'twoer' becoming a 'tenner' by defeating an 'eighter'. No match I suppose for an X Box (whatever that is) or indeed a Game Boy or any Ap on their mobile phone. You see today's child with eyes transfixed to these, with only the flickering of their pupils and the twitching of thumbs to denote that they are still alive. The black arts of conker hardening may well be lost forever but today's kids are probably a bit more hi-tec and could devise their own formulas, perhaps injecting their conkers with resin or some carbon fibre concoction to create an indestructible 'super conker'.

What I find particularly sad though, is not the demise of the game of conkers itself – but the fact that the kids took any notice of the ban. In my day, such an edict would have given the game extra kudos. The bike sheds, always the venue for illicit smoking, would have been the grandstand for the outlawed conker.

Original US poster.

A Film Premier in Blackpool.
Introducing 'Emergo'

You've probably never even heard of Emergo (pronounced Emerge-O), the entertainment wonder introduced to the British cinemagoer in 1958. Possibly because 1958 was also the year of Emergo's very predictable 'Disappear-O'.

I was an art student in Blackpool at the time this new cinema sensation was to be launched direct from America with a film called House on Haunted Hill. Quite a coup for a local cinema to host a Premier and to publicise the event the enterprising local manager of the Princess Cinema (now closed) approached the art school with the idea that the graphics department (then known as commercial design) could create posterdesigns by way of a competition.

Getting art students to produce any work at all in that department was a major task, but strangely enough the idea caught the collective imagination and quite an exhibition of appropriately ghoulish designs subsequently adorned the cinema foyer. The winning design featured a grinning scull with a spooky silhouette house in the background. It was conceived by my friend Spike. Unfortunately (or perhaps fortunately) no record exists of Spikes masterpiece. I think this was the pinnacle of his artistic career as he dropped out of art school shortly after and disappeared out of our lives without a trace. That was, until just a few days before writing this, that I got an email from the long lost Spike who was living on the Isle of Skye and running a bagpipe museum. Life as they say, is stranger than fiction.

It was Spike who reminded me again of this whole affair, telling me his prize was two tickets to see the film. Not much of a prize when you consider all the other poster designers also got one free ticket. On the other hand, he was able to treat some girl to a night out at the cinema, even though the film of choice was rather less than romantic. Still, it was a 'Premier'.

I have to admit that most of our designs were done with tongue in cheek, probably just as well really. Had we attempted to do something with 'taste' in the graphic style of the day, we would probably have failed miserably. As it was, it turned out to be an appropriately display of macabre images to suitably promote the event.

The film itself was absolutely forgettable, I even had to consult a film guide to tell me what it was all about. What did surprise me was that it was described as a 'classic' and had starred Vincent Price. It had also been awarded three stars. The catalogue blurb also mentioned that it had introduced Emergo to the American public. This was of course prior to its dramatic British launch in 1958.

To the poster designers, Emergo was still under wraps (or shrouds) but it unintentionally partly revealed itself as soon as we entered the cinema. To
the right of the screen there was a large coffin fixed to the wall. Protruding from over the top of which were wires strung above the audience and back to the projection room, similar to the cash systems you used to see in the old Co-ops. It was pretty obvious that whatever Emergo was, it was going to emerge from here and the whole audience was waiting for it to happen. The surprise element was non-existent but there was the excitement of anticipation.

At an appropriate creepy climax in the film, Emergo sprung (well creaked) into inaction. The coffin lid swung open and a replica skeleton jiggled and jerked its way along the very visible wires above the audience. Instead of the intended screams, the whole place erupted with laughter and howls of derision. The audience were armed and ready, bombarding the unfortunate skeleton was with ice cream cartons, chewing gum, popcorn and whatever else could be hurled. The Emergo skeleton scuttled back out of the spotlight to its coffin refuge, safe from this scary world - never to be seen again. In showbiz terms – it died.

It still raises a laugh when we recall it, and only recently when I spoke to another old art school colleague, he told me that he and his mates in the fine art department had made the thing from papier-mâché, wood and bits of wire all under a cloak of secrecy.

Now sixty years on, I think the time is right for Re-Emergo. Perhaps this time promoted as a comedy film. It could become a cult thing like the Rocky Horror Show and everyone could dress up as skeletons and perform the Emergo dance in the aisles. On the other hand, perhaps its demise was appropriate.

It was a 'first' for Blackpool though.

"I've invented a new camouflage material."

Winter wonderland

Long ago, in the last millennium, I was a very small boy scout. Those were the days when we wore strange khaki felt hats with flat brims and the crown pinched in to form a point. A ludicrous legacy from the Baden-Powel era.

I have a photograph of my father as a scout also wearing one with a brim far flatter than I could ever achieve. In fact none of my contemporaries had a flat brim - they all came with a variety of wave effects.
One lad I recall had a distinctive decorative edge to his brim by courtesy of his pet hamster and mine was a disgrace having followed dubious advice from a 'friend'. I'd been advised that ironing the brim sprinkled with sugar would create a firm, flat effect to be the envy of all on church parade. The only thing worse than the subsequent state of my brim was my mum's iron.

I can thank scouting for introducing me to a variety of skills from first aid to semaphore, most of which has been lost in the recesses of my memory banks. We also learnt Morse code but I can only recall the three dots - three dashes - three dots of SOS and the single dot of E. So I can at least still flash a torch if I get stuck on a hill - or ESSO on my headlights if I run out of petrol. I could probably also administer a tourniquet to anyone with a severed artery, though I would probably cause the patient to lose a limb.

However, I will always be indebted to my days in the scout movement for my introduction to the Lake District and to this day I can clearly recall my first expedition - the Fairfield round in a snowstorm.

Looking back I can't think why anyone in their right mind would take a party of young lads up Fairfield with a snowstorm imminent but I suppose they were different days and safety wasn't the priority it is today. Having said that, I still read in the *Westmoreland Gazette* of people getting lost or stranded on the fells having set out in the most atrocious conditions.

To us it was just a big adventure and we were oblivious to the dangers. Whether or not our leader was, I'll never know. By the time we'd reached Hart Crag the snow was swirling thick and fast and it was decided that we should all be roped together. This was Everest; we were at the cutting edge of mountain peak conquest. We were probably at the edge of a few other things too but we were unaware. All we could see was each other, and snow.
It's strange how some images stay in your mind and I can recall seeing the boys roped in front of me as we picked our way through the whiteness. No doubt, had our trusted leader ventured over one of the precipitous drops, we would have all followed like a string of lemmings.

As it was we emerged at the end of the day, excited, thrilled and quite unscathed. Doubtless our leader was relieved that it was all over. How he'd known which way to go I've no idea, and I suspect he didn't either.

Winter is a great season for walking the fells. They really do look at their dramatic best when capped with snow against a cloud free blue sky. To be up there on the ridges on a crystal clear day is a real treat. The silence can be quite strange with just the crunch of the snow under your boots. Even the becks and waterfalls are silenced in an icy grip.

There's an extra sense of adventure too when the paths are covered with snow and you have to negotiate your own route over the fells. And it can be great fun. I once came across a young chap with his girlfriend who had a small, easy to carry sledge. Basically it was just a round plastic tray with a handle at the front. You sat on the tray with your feet out in front - and you were away. Fantastic. We created our own Cresta Run down towards Grisedale Tarn. There's nothing like snow for bringing out the child in you. Snow on the fells is wonderful, but snow clouds themselves should be left well alone. There must de countless tales of dodgy situations in the snow, some of course with tragic consequences. I often walk alone and I try to avoid bad weather anyway, but snowstorms pose the greatest danger. The problem is they can travel so quickly. I once observed one from the fells above Hartsop. It appeared to just roll in like a giant snowball across the Helvellyn range. Anyone caught on Striding Edge certainly wouldn't have been striding as it went through.

On another occasion I was caught at the top of a snow covered Wetherlam Edge by a flurry of snowflakes which rapidly changed into quite a heavy fall of snow. I decided to retrace my own footprints and thus avoid disappearing down one of the many old copper mine shafts which are normally fairly easy to spot (if you know they are there). Within minutes my tracks were re-covered with fresh snow and my way down back to Tilberthwaite was only aided by my knowledge of the area. In this instance I was not in any particular danger but I did reflect that had I not been on familiar ground, I could have been. I certainly wouldn't have liked to have been in charge of a group of boy scouts in such a situation.

A friend recounted to me how he and a group of experienced fell walkers were once caught in a severe snowstorm and completely lost their bearings. They decided to head for the relative safety of low ground and struggled through waist high drifts, eventually finding themselves in Langstrath rather than Langdale where they'd left their car. They had to spend the night at a hotel in Borrowdale.

Early this year I came across some steps cut into a steep section of snow on Fairfield as I came up from the direction of St Sunday Crag. Some kind soul must have been demonstrating how to use an ice axe and it certainly saved me an awkward scramble. In fact I would never have made it up that particular slope unaided. I've often thought it would be worth learning how to use one properly.

I did buy a pair of crampons for walking on the fells when the snow is deep and hard packed but I've never had occasion yet to use them. I don't think normal boots are up to the job. The problem is that I always think you need to be a serious mountaineer to warrant crampons or use an ice axe and I'd probably feel a bit of a poser. Better to be safe than sorry though, as they say. My advice to anyone venturing onto snow-covered fells is simple. Be careful - or better still- 'be prepared'. Now there's a motto for you. As a footnote (if you pardon the pun) since writing this little piece, I have had occasion to try my crampons. They were brilliant on those high fell paths that winter conditions turn into mini Cresta runs.

Splish, splash, clunk.

Some years ago, in a fit of enthusiasm I purchased a Canadian style canoe. The craft was duly taken up to my caravan in the Lakes and lay there gathering bird droppings and creating a habitat for all manner of crawling things. It even became a shelter for an orphaned lamb which slept under it at night.

The idea was of course that it would be launched, straight away but other things kept cropping up and the maiden voyage was put back - and the months went by. My wife didn't actually say much about the expense (I'm relieved to say) but she did begin to murmur about the fact that its landlocked state was something of a waste. Its official launch date was hurriedly fixed for the next available sunny day.

And so, on a calm morning, I slid silently out from Brown Howe on the West shore of Coniston Water onto the still surface of the lake as the early morning sun was just making its presence felt. Only a few early - rising campers were breaking the silence.

One of the advantages of the open canoe is its ability to carry weight. I suppose originally some outback trapper would have lashed a dead moose on board and set off down the rapids. My moose equivalent was a large plastic box containing all manner of things I would probably never use and enough food for a 'Famous Five' picnic.

As a newcomer to canoeing I was pleased that it was so calm as I made my way across the lake using a double bladed kayak paddle rather than the correct single bladed one. The canoe is slightly wider than the kayak and this was the only thing that spoilt my steady rhythm as the paddle occasionally caught the side with a clunk and the resulting splashes soon had me wet through.

My voyage of discovery took me across to Peel Island, and in true explorer's style I circumnavigated it. This great undertaking took about two minutes and I was back in the middle of the lake, very wet, but at one with my new adventurous world.

By this time a number of other craft had appeared. Some were being used for fishing and a couple of motorboats had made their way up from the hire point at Coniston. From Peel Island it's about two and a half miles to Coniston. So, having enjoyed the fine views of the fells, tucked into a few sandwiches and removed most of my excess wet items, I decided to venture up the lake in that direction.

The long, narrow design of the canoe is such that it will cut through the water quite easily and smoothly, even in the hands of a novice, and it didn't take me long to splish, splash and clunk my way up to the jetty at Coniston.

There area was quite busy with people preparing for an antique 'working boat' regatta and they were taking to the becalmed waters with their optimistic sails hanging limply. Even with no wind in their sails these craft are a delight. Decades of purely functional design have created beautiful lines to the hulls and viewed with the cut of their sales they create a perfect balance of shapes that any artist would be satisfied to achieve.

I tried to catch what little wind there was is my own makeshift spinnaker - my umbrella (one of the items I thought I would never use) hoping to drift back down the lake, but with no luck. It was quicker to splish, splash, clunk and I'd soon left the little flotilla well behind.

About three quarters of the way the wind began to get up - a south wind, of course, so I was unable to use it with my umbrella. It also became quite difficult to keep the craft in a straight line with the wind trying to turn it either left or right. This had the effect of introducing more 'clunks' into my disturbed rhythm and consequently more splashes. Eventually I reached my launch point by use of brute strength and frantic paddling.

Brown Howe is a popular launching site and I met a group of experienced canoeists about to take to the water. Enthusiasts in any activity are always keen to impart their enthusiasm and offer advice to newcomers and I was given plenty of useful information.
I've even learned how to travel upwind. It's all down to weight distribution and one's paddling position. If you paddle from the near front of the canoe, the weather-vane effect blows the craft into line - It's as simple as that! The enthusiasts were local chaps and they told me that one of their favourite trips was to negotiate the River Crake that runs out of the south foot of Coniston and down to Greenod and the sea. I'm not sure that my current canoe, being simply of fibreglass construction, is up to the task. Come to think of it, probably neither am I. Yet.

You can actually convert an open canoe into a 'sailing' craft. I'm told that a well handled sailing canoe can embarrass a small dinghy for speed. I think the key phrase here is 'well handled' as stability would appear to be the factor in question.

My initiation into the world of canoeing was over - and it wasn't just a case of re-enacting the 'Last of the Mohicans' - I'd become a real life 'redskin'. Having failed to take account of the sun's strength I spent the next couple of very painful weeks with bright, lobster-red legs.

Dangerous and foolish, I know, but I've learnt my lesson and I'm *heap sorry*, I can tell you.

Luxury motoring

In the late 50s I was an art student, which enabled me to enjoy the fun-filled world of further education without the actual education. Life was wonderful but, like most students, I was skint. However, I was lucky enough to receive £20 on my birthday from a wealthy aunt. With this and another £5 I'd scrambled together I was for a fleeting moment rich to the tune of £25.

My mother always told me that money burns a hole in my pocket and I have to admit it's true, but in my defense, who could resist a 1932 Austin 7 saloon with red leather bucket seats for £25?

I never serviced it, I didn't know a con rod from a fishing rod and I only put oil in it if I had some. When it comes to cars I never wanted to know what goes on under the bonnet - as long as it just goes on, going on. The little 7 served me well and started every time, though it often needed coaxing with a starting handle.

One Sunday I took my long-suffering girl friend Helene (now my even longer suffering wife) to the Lakes in it. She'd never been to the Lake District before and bought a pair of stout shoes and an anorak for the trip. "I'll take you up Helvellyn," I'd declared a few days before and showed her on the map. This didn't mean a thing to her of course but she went along with my enthusiasm.

We set off from her home in Blackpool, my little Austin 7 nibbling away at the pre motorway miles up through

Garstang, Lancaster and eventually making it to Kendal. On the steep rise leaving town Helene had to get out and walk alongside as the little car was feeling the strain, and so was she. On we plodded through Stavely and at last we came over the final brow and she caught her first glimpse of Windermere.

It was always a magic moment when I was a young lad to get that view of the lake. That's when you knew you'd arrived. For weeks you'd been looking forward to your holiday, and there it was before you. Straight ahead were all your favourite fells and peaks. Now you were back in Lakeland. On we went and Helene was enjoying the scenery. We drove straight on passing through Ambleside and by Grasmere and up the steady climb of Dunmail Rise. The little car must have got its second wind as Helene didn't have to get out again even though it's quite a long hard slog up there. We made it to the top and cruised down (if you can cruise in an Austin 7) to a car park by the little chapel at Wythburn.

Off we went through the forest and up the open fellside into a rather disappointing low cloud. I was trying to explain what a wonderful view you could have from the summit on a clear day - but I don't think I was winning my case. She wasn't used to fell walking and was getting tired and damp. She'd also been sitting in a tiny Austin 7 for several hours.
Suddenly, as though by some divine intervention, the clouds lifted and there before us was the Lake District at its wonderful dramatic best. We enjoyed our picnic, her faith in me was almost restored and we happily returned to our car. Driving home again was a doddle, well, it's virtually down hill all the way from Helvellyn to Blackpool isn't it?

It's a pity I didn't hang on to that little Austin, it would be worth a few quid these days. Back then it was just another old car. Cute, but you wouldn't have thought of it as an investment. I certainly didn't. There was one fellow student who would have known then, and that was a chap called Jim. I met Jim again some years later when we were colleagues at a large advertising agency. By that time Jim was quite well known in the veteran and vintage car world and was chairman of his local club. He attended rallies all over the place and invited me and another chap from the studio to join him on a rally in the Lakes.

Jim owned a few vehicles but the sporty little number he was taking was a little Morris - very similar to my old Austin 7. "It's a McEvoy Special," he informed us proudly (I think that's what he called it). It was a convertible too as I recall; ideal for Lakeland touring - in good weather. We were lucky, it only drizzled a bit.

The organisers of these events really put the old cars through their paces, and they don't mess about. I think they treat them with real respect, that is as tough working machines rather than pretty, delicate ones. They certainly don't mollycoddle them. Half the time I hadn't got a clue what was going on. We were given map references and had checkpoints to pass, but it wasn't just a case of blasting round the Lakeland lanes at speed. These checkpoints had to be reached at a time nearest to what maintaining a constant average speed would achieve.
Get it? Well I didn't. Well, I sort of did, but not really how you did it. So I just sat back and enjoyed the views.

What those rally boys needed was one of those hand- held satellite navigation devices.

A friend of mine told me the other day that he tapes one onto the A frame of his motorised hang glider. It not only gives him his altitude but his ground speed and average speed. He'd also tried it out on a land yacht in America earlier in the year. Over there they sail on dry lakes in the desert and position the turning marks several miles apart. By simply tapping in the co-ordinates, the device showed him exactly which direction to go - and it's apparently within the rules. He said they had great fun with it as it plotted their every move.

Great for walking in the Lakes on a bad day. The only time a walker using one need worry is when the altitude reading suddenly changes rapidly. This would indicate they'd entered a faulty map reference and they were in fact over a cliff. Today's rally types are probably already on to this and are reaching all the checkpoints right on the button.

Eventually, after various trials involving manoeuvring around fields and up bumpy farm lanes, we reached a point at the top of Honister Pass where I realised there was a hidden agenda. We passengers were there for a reason. We were ballast.

There's a very steep track running from the pass up to the Honister Slate Quarry. Our task was to stand on the running boards and jump up and down to create traction as the little Morris tried to get as far up the slope as it could.

I chose the side nearest to the fell, naturally, and we shot forward with the engine racing at a million rpm, and not being quiet about it. Old McEvoy (or whatever his name was) would have been doing similar revolutions in his grave if he'd had any idea what his little special was to be put through. This along with two passengers hanging on to the sides and jumping up and down trying to look like expert traction men.

It gave up the ghost about half way, accompanied by the strange smell of burning, or at least something was a lot hotter than it should have been.

The next car up in our class was a little Austin 7 (not my old one) which shot past us and disappeared up the quarry for maximum points. Of course Jim told us later that he should have replaced the clutch with a new one before the event but thought it would have been all right. We weren't complete failures as traction men after all.

I've been motoring in the Lake District for decades and it's still an enjoyable experience but it's not getting any easier. Cars are getting faster and patience shorter - and Continental style coaches bigger and bigger. Take those little country lanes around Sawrey in midsummer where 70 years ago two ponies and traps meeting head on would have been regarded as gridlock. Now we have coaches that look big even on our motorways. I'm certainly tempted to use local transport when I'm off for a day's fell walking.

Perhaps my own view is spoilt by memories of more carefree days when I could trundle through the Lakes in an Austin 7 and not only be the lone car in a Lake District car park but also be the lone walkers on Helvellyn.

You can get gridlocked on Striding Edge these days.

Strictly come shuffling.

I can't really dance.

Having said that, I can shuffle my way round any dance floor. It's really quite simple, left foot, right foot together, right foot left foot together - repeat and repeat till the music stops. This is a universal dance step system which carried me through my teenage years at numerous village and church halls in the 1950s.

The dance protocol followed a simple format which had miraculously stood the test of time for decades. Initially all the girls would take their seats against the walls surrounding the dance floor and the lads would stand in a huddle at one end of the room. The M.C's announcements would usually be a disembodied voice from behind a curtain which would always follow a very formal routine – 'Please take your partners for a foxtrot', or a quickstep or whatever, and the record would start to play.

It could be anything from the hit parade of the day, Dickie Valentine, Alma Cogan, Lita Rosa etc. Slowly, and due to a lack of male response, one or two girls would get up and dance together. Some girls who were a bit more dance savvy would actually perform the dance with legitimate steps around the floor. Others would resort to my afore mentioned shuffle routine.

The next dance would be announced and the process repeated, perhaps with one or two lads who had steady girlfriends joining in. This move would give courage to other lads who would target a girl of their choice and trot out the traditional request, 'Please may I have the pleasure of this dance?' No one ever questioned this phrase or deviated from it. This was how dance requests had always been done. The chosen girl would usually accept and the couple would proceed to shuffle around the floor until the record finished. Thank-yous were exchanged and the couples would return to their previous stations.

Dance organizers had other schemes to get couples on the floor. One such was the Paul Jones in which the girls would form a ring in the centre of the floor and an equal number of lads would eventually and after a bit of cajoling, form another ring around them. When the music started each ring would move in opposite directions till it stopped and you were stuck with, or silently rejoiced in the partner directly in front of you. The music would continue and the shuffling would commence. A complete lottery, but it relieved any shy male from having to ask for a dance.

Who was this Paul Jones anyway? I had to consult Google for the answer to this burning question. He was an 18th Century American Naval Officer from the time of the American Revolution. He may have been a gallant, decorated officer but his legacy is to the world of dance, (reason still unknown) and perhaps responsible for millions of romances, successful or otherwise.

Other anachronistic dance forms were played out as the evening progressed. 'Take your partners please for The Gay Gordons' – The Military two-step, The Highland Reel, The Barn Dance. You certainly couldn't shuffle to these but there were no real complicated steps to master and once you'd seen the routine it was easy to just follow. After a few beers they can become quite raucous affairs.

By the mid to late 50s, something of a revolution was occurring in the music world and rock and roll records were taking over the charts. Dance organizers had to allow slots for this and jiving was the new dance craze. This gave lads new confidence as it allowed them to be more macho with their dance moves an they were less reluctant to approach partners. Gradually these jive slots became longer and other dance forms left the floor. How they ever lasted so long is quite amazing but we post war teenagers were a new demographic. Prior to this once someone had left school they went into employment and were simply young adults.

More teenagers also went to College or even University but we were a new force. We didn't actually rebel against those antiquated dances, they had their benefits. They were 'contact' dances. A chance to get really close to a girl with your arm around her. Where else could you do this but on a dance floor? You didn't even have to learn to dance. The shuffle just became shorter and you could even do it on the spot with a rhythmic sway.

Another benefit was the age-old tradition of the 'Last Waltz'. This was also a lad's last chance. If you could find a partner for this you were half way to making your evening successful. They would often turn the lights down too as a romantic gesture and couples could shuffle away to the music in close embrace. This was the moment you could ask a girl if you could walk her home. Something of a euphemism but nearly always, even if she agreed to your offer, ended up with just a walk home – we lads always lived in hope.

Occasionally, dance organizers had a live band take to the

stage for a free concert. No one would dance but everyone

would crowd round at the front of the stage whist they
went through their play list. My friends and I did this
ourselves when we had a skiffle group. We had lots of fun
but looking back, I'm sure most folk would have preferred
to carry on dancing (or shuffling). Every band would always
have at least one sequence where each individual member
would have his moment of glory with a solo. This is fine
but it always included the drummer, regardless of his ability.
We would stand for what seemed like an eternity whilst
some guy performed his impression of a bin lorry being
loaded - then to rapturous applause. I never really
understood that.

The current television series of "Strictly come Dancing'
may well inspire more people to learn to dance. I can
recall going to a dinner dance in France some years ago
where the parents of a friend took to the dance floor and
tangoed their way to massive applause. She was small and
round and certainly not built to tango, but they were step
perfect. I was quite impressed. Perhaps if I just learned to
execute one dace such as the tango it could be my party
piece. Folk would assume that you had a whole repertoire
of dances anyway. I once did some drawings for an article
in the Oldie about the Tango. Apparently, it was originally a
dance for two males in Argentina. Not really what I had in
mind.

I have another friend who goes Salsa dancing. On his
seventieth birthday he held a party and invited all his
friends along. All his Salsa friends turned up too. Beautiful
young Philipino girls all eager to dance the night away with
him. No shuffling here. This was tricky stuff but obviously

there were real benefits. My friend though is single and I'm not sure my wife would go along with these dance lessons.

In the meantime, may I have the pleasure of the next shuffle?

Pouring cold water on a theory.

Far be it for me to suggest that ancient Brits were not a clever bunch of fellows when it came to erecting stone monuments via ramps, rollers or whatever method they employed. But when it comes to claims about the movement of some giant stones two hundred and fifty miles I have to raise a questioning eyebrow – or two.

I read that for example the famous 'blue stones' at Stonehenge came from South Wales – each weighing in at some 4 tonnes. That of course is a geological fact, but if they cared for such blue stones so much, wouldn't it have easier to build the thing in South Wales? Besides, who discovered them? Was it a weekend away to Wales and someone said, 'These look nice, much better than the stuff we've got locally, lets carry them home, it'll only take years.'

Some other stones there have come twenty-five miles down the road and they weigh in at – wait for it - fifty tonnes a throw. Apparently the manpower for this little D.I.Y. job is estimated to run into a few hundred, and I'm not sure if they had horsepower to help out in those days.

Twenty-five miles, well, ok, I accept that it's possible, but is it probable.

There are dozens of stone circles dotted around Ireland and Great Britain, along with rows of stones and what have you, but the predominant arrangement is in a circle. They come in all sizes and in odd places.

Now, here's a little experiment I've devised to give you a clue how I think a lot of these came about. It may or may not explain Stonehenge – but who really knows anyway. My theory is as good as any.

Right. Take a Tupperware container and half fill it with water. Stick it in your freezer until frozen. Then scatter some stone chippings or pebbles from you garden on the top, top up the container up with more water and pop it back in the freezer. Eventually you'll end up with a replication of stones encapsulated in a glacier such as covered Britain in the Glacial Age. A glacier that was almost a mile deep in places. Its pebbles could have been, and were, any size it wanted. Fifty tonnes, no problem. This phenomenon transported rocks almost from one end of the country to the other and dropped them willy-nilly when it melted. You can replicate this movement by popping down the road to your brother in law's with your little tub, but it's much easier to simply place it in the garden. Then, as the ice melts the stones slide outwards from the centre, it's a combination of weight and the sun warming up the stones, as it melts they eventually form a stone ring. Hardly any stones end up in the centre. The point is, any stones collected together, were deposited together, they didn't move about in the ice.

Now, if you were an ancient Brit, or whoever first

encountered these isles, you would chance upon this strange formation of stones and declare it a mystical place. Anything we can't explain we attribute to the God's. That's been the way of the world.

Our ancient forbears wouldn't have found a perfect circle, but it only takes a bloke with two pegs and the equivalent of a ball of string to mark that out. The point is, he had a ready-made area that looked a bit on the spooky side - surrounded by stones.

There's probably someone out there who will tell me my little theory doesn't hold water – even frozen water. He or she may well be right, you can carry on believing that those giant stones came by roller and barge if you want, you can even believe they were dropped by a flying saucer.

I know that different activities occurred at different periods at Stonehenge, but it doesn't mean all the stones weren't there to begin with – that's probably why they chose the site for the first place. I think my theory about those stones stacks up, even if I don't know how those ancient Brits eventually managed to actually stack 'em up.

Kings of the Mountains

Imagine if you were to place a sizeable hill in the middle of somewhere like, say, East Anglia. You would evoke all manner of reactions.

Leaving aside the bloke who would buy it, fence it off and erect a sign saying 'PRIVATE – KEEP OUT', you would get others who would simply recognise it for its building development value.

Others would want to work it, drill holes in it and mine it, blast lumps off it, forest it or farm it and let sheep roam all over it. You would also get The Ministry of Defence buzzing it with jets (it sounds just like the Lake District in microcosm).

There are people who would just admire it and possibly photograph it. Others may be inspired to create poetry and some write about it. Artists would include it in a landscape.

Then you get the group who would see its potential for leisure activities. Some would want to fly off it, ski on it or climb all over it. Ramblers would simply want to walk up it to enjoy the views it offered over East Anglia. Last but not least you would get that hardy bunch who would want to run straight up it and down the other side. Wherever you have a hill - you'll find the hill runner, or in northern climes, the fell runner.

In Lakeland where the fells are larger and the terrain rockier the fell runners are at the 'peak' of their sport. A different breed in fact from normal cross country runners, and their skills grant them exemption from the safety rules observed by mere fell walkers.

Alfred Wainwright could never get his head round fell running and dismissed the sport. He would savour every step and believed that you couldn't enjoy the fell or the view if you were doing it on the run. He once observed. that he never saw a fell runner smiling whilst running . Well that's not surprising is it - and just how many walkers walk about with a smile. I reckon half the time I'm out walking I'm grimacing. Much as I admire his work I think he was the blinkered one. Of course the fell runner loves the fells just as much as anyone.

I've come across these hardy souls all over the place on the fells. Some time you will see a group actually taking part in a fell race or training for a big event like the Bob Graham round , a mind numbingly gruelling , 72 peaks in 24 hours. You just can't help but admire some of these feats.

Once as I was making my way off Great Gable, a stony place if ever there was one. The only vegetation up there is on the withered leaves of the wreaths placed on the memorial plaque every November. I was heading West to make my way down the boulder strewn path and then on to Kirk Fell. A lone fell runner padded past. He was in his late70s or even 80s, slightly built and wearing vest , shorts and trainers. He glanced at his obligatory fell runner's watch then took a swig from his water bottle, the only other item he carried.

By the time I was half way down Gable I could see him half way up Kirk. His almost mechanical step didn't falter as he skipped from rock to rock. He was probably rushing home in time to get his pension from the Post Office.

I can really appreciate just how good the fell runner is because I once had a feeble go at it.

Years ago I used to be a runner. Not a fell runner or even a distance runner, though I did complete a Marathon once to prove something to myself. I was a sprinter - a different discipline altogether. Glancing through an athletics magazine I spotted an ad for The Grasmere Sports. Thinking that it would be great just to take part in such a historic event I quickly sent off my entry.

The Grasmere Sports covers a variety of events from the traditional Cumberland Wrestling (I'm still not sure why they wear embroidered underpants) to hound trailing, a real Lake District speciality. There are track events in the arena including sprints (or dashes) and culminating in the Grasmere Sports big event - The Guide Race for the fell runners.

The sprint races were for cash prizes and I noticed quite a few of the competitors were from Scotland and the North East. I figured that there must be some kind of race 'circuit' as they seemed to know each other. I was an unknown quantity and placed on the 'scratch' line for a 90 yard race, giving some chaps about ten yards . The handicap system ensured that I certainly didn't win but I wasn't actually last . I was only really there for the experience of taking part anyway. Later I ran in a race around the circuit, about 400 yards, and was lucky enough to be amongst the number that received a small £5 cash prize designed to cover expenses.

Can you believe I worried for weeks that by accepting the £5 I had compromised my amateur status. And to think what today's 'amateurs' are earning.

The hound trail was quite a highlight. The 'trail' had been laid previously by someone dragging an aniseed soaked sack for miles across the fells which the hounds were to follow. It occurs to me that stray dogs could be rounded up by the same technique.

The hounds duly bounded off yelping with their respective owners urging them on. Some minutes later they were spotted miles away on the crest of a fell. It's a bit like going to the dog track but with the dogs leaving the stadium and tearing around the town before coming back in for the big finish. In this case the big finish is a real noisy affair. The owners standing on the finishing line, each trying to out shout the other. The dogs bounded in still running flat out after covering mile after mile of fell country. If you're ever faced with an angry dog. My advice is don't even think about running. Either face it and fight it - or negotiate!!

Finally the moment came for the Guide Race and the competitors left the the start line in the centre of the show ground arena, crossed the road and headed straight up the fell side. A guide race is relatively short in fell running terms. It took the leading runners about 12 minutes to reach the turning marker at the top, and just 2 minutes to return. The leader sprinted back over the road, cross the line in some style and was duly feted. He was the local hero for another year.

When the whole affair was over and spectators were drifting away I decided to try my hand (or should that be feet) at fell running. I didn't have the experience or to tell the truth bottle to actually enter the race. But now I could give it a go. I trotted across the road and made my way up the fell. Slowly. I didn't do too badly as I was fairly fit at the time and was only reduced to walking pace on a couple of sections - but then so had some of the 'official' runners. Eventually I reached the turning point and stood for a while quite out of breath.

Now, this is where my appreciation for the fell runners stems from - the descent. They had made it from top to bottom in just 2 fantastic, broken limb defying minutes. Going up the fell depends on your level of fitness, going down is dependent on your level of lunacy. I just came down with care, the care of a fell walker.

At one point I reached a stone wall which I recalled the runners had just launched themselves at , and with one foot on the wall they were airborne again. I couldn't do that, self preservation came first I'm afraid ('afraid' is a rather apt word). Even out walking I wear strong boots to protect my ankles. A fell run for me would surely end with a hospital visit.

Eventually I reached the foot of the fell, level ground at last. I wasn't now subject to the laws of gravity that cover rolling stones. I could stop when I chose to - but I didn't. I jogged across the road and back into the show ground.

Having completed the course, albeit in a rather slow time, I still felt a sense of achievement. My appreciation for the stamina and sheer nerve of the fell runner was confirmed. In Tour de France terms - fell runners are truly Kings of the Mountains.

Sales Tales

We all know that supermarkets have all manner of sophisticated schemes involving store layout, traffic flow, where and how items are displayed, and all designed obviously to empty shelves and fill our baskets. To a supermarket, shelves are more akin to aircraft carrier decks, products must fly off them – or they could be ditched.

To a product manufacturer, getting listed with a supermarket is only half the battle, you have to stay listed. Losing a contract with a big store group could upset your whole apple cart. I designed some packs years ago for a small time tea company. The Sales Director confided in me (he was proud of his dubious exploits) how he'd raided the rubbish bins of his main competitor (his previous employer) to extract the computer printouts. This gave him the exact blend details of tea they were promoting and at what price. He was then able to undercut them and on one occasion, he purchased a smallish store's complete stock of tea to replace it with his own identical product. He later re-packed the tea in his own boxes and sold it on.
All that just to get listed.
The supermarket holds all the cards, and sales are trumps. When you see those 'Two for the price of one' offers, it's the manufacturer who foots the bill. All manner of sales promotions offering deals, prizes, money off, are put forward by the manufacturer to help shift his product, and keep the supermarket sweet.

I worked for a couple of very successful ex-colleagues from advertising who set up a sales promotion business. Sales promotion covers a variety of activities and is an area that most advertising agencies don't get involved in, they can burn their fingers. It's a game where you have to know all the numbers. For example, if product X wanted to have an on-pack offer of a football at a discount price. You'd have to source the football, perhaps printed with a special logo, order the right amount (at the right price) and not be left with any at the end of the day. And, hopefully increase the sales of product X to keep it flying off the shelves. Pretty tall order. Failure, don't even think about it.

In terms of percentages, these sales increases are quite small, but they could translate quite well in terms of volume. Also a lot of on-pack offers are picked up but not taken up. You need to be able to forecast what those conversions are going to be, or you could end up with a warehouse full of footballs or worse still, a load of unhappy, complaining, football-less customers.

The two chaps I worked for had this game off to a T. They worked hard and made plenty – and good luck to them. They took all the risks. By this time in my career I was just Joe Bloggs in the corner of their studio, a mere observer of all this frenetic activity and just helping out a couple of days a week with a few images or design work they needed to source quickly. The studio itself was just a bank of Apple Macs clicking away the day. Everything is high speed and highly undesirable.

They had a working relationship with another company that had the ultimate, cash register ringing, sales promotion scheme – Die-Cast metal vehicles. These were produced in any livery and offered on pack at a discount price. The promotion company received a management fee (ker-ching), a fee depending on the number of packs carrying the offer (ker-ching) and a mark-up on the die-cast vehicles (ker-ching). On top of this Mr Die-Cast had a collectors' Club that snapped all the left over vehicles (ker-ching). A brilliant business model – so to speak.

The chaps I worked for decided to emulate this idea with one of their own featuring miniature resin Teddy Bears. Joe Bloggs was of course, the designer of the bears which were then modelled by someone else and eventually being knocked out and painted for pence in the Far East.

I must have designed hundreds of Teddy Bears for all manner of companies and products. Each Teddy came in its own miniature box accompanied with a little leaflet about its life. Some of things I've turned my designer's hand to, if it wasn't funny it would be shameful.

 Those Teddies were successful in terms of getting a foot in the door of major companies and the promotions worked well, unfortunately the collectors club didn't reach the number required to always clear the left overs. Shame really, it was a good idea, though I wasn't sad to see the last Teddy off my drawing board. I could draw Teddy families in my sleep.

"It's my mobile home."

Corporal Stupid

Having enjoyed a variety of canoes and touring kayaks over the last few years I fancied something with a bit of speed. I found the very thing on eBay. Sprint kayak 'Buy it Now' £150 O.N.O. For readers unfamiliar with the wonders of eBay, 'Buy it Now' is basically what it says on the tin. There is no auction. I put in an offer of £100, thinking that's as much as I want to pay, bearing in mind it would have to be collected some sixty miles away. My offer was accepted and a few days later I was the owner of a sprint kayak albeit out of date for the current generation of sprint kayakers.

As it tuned out, it wasn't a sprint kayak, but an Olympic slalem kayak.
My new toy was in super condition. Especially bearing in mind its age. I figured it must have spent the bulk of its life, in someone's garage. It's incredibly light, being constructed I think, from Kevlar, an extra light kind of glass fibre. This suited me even more. My current two seater touring kayak weighs something akin to Titanic and there's no way I can get it on a roof rack, I have to use a trailer. This new speed machine can be held aloft without even gritting my teeth.
I couldn't wait to launch it and rushed up to my usual site in the Lakes. I knew it was quick from the first couple of strokes and soon I was ripping down the river. This is a flat-water river; I'm not into the white water stuff. Nothing against it, I've never tried it, besides, I really quite enjoy a day out on a lake with an on board picnic and a flask.

My feeling that it was quick was confirmed when a young chap in another kayak asked we what kind of kayak it was. He'd not been able to stay with it and his was a sort of hybrid touring-cum-sprint design. Don't ask me to explain, all these designs are a mystery to me too really.

When it comes to kayaking I've always had an idea in the back of my mind to get a sea kayak. This is a specially designed craft to cope with waves, not a toy by any means, something you don't do on your own and never without proper training. This statement makes me sound rather like Captain Sensible - but the truth is, I can, and often do, become my alter-ego, Corporal Stupid.

My newfound speedy device was a fairly stable little craft, unlike some, which can be very tippy. Even so, I thought I'd better learn a kayak skill,
which most kayakers learn as youngsters – the Eskimo roll. If I wanted to progress to a sea kayak it would be essential. So, back to the computer and on to You Tube. Type anything in on You Tube and you get loads of film clips from around the world showing you how it's done. The Eskimo roll looked a doddle. From an indicated starting position under water you simply sweep your paddle across the surface until you are horizontal, a quick flip of the hip and up you come, bringing the heaviest part of your body, your head, up last. Bingo, the Eskimo roll. Film clips showed kids doing it with their hands – look no paddle. Corporal Stupid was set for action.

A couple of days later found him sitting in his speed machine at the side of the river practicing his underwater paddle action. Then at the side of the riverbank his hip flick technique was honed to perfection. Time to put all this to the test.

Corporal stupid paddled to the centre of the river. There is a bend in the river at this point and the flow of water coming from the lake can be quite swift after heavy rain. This was of course following heavy rain. Setting himself, Corporal Stupid went through his Eskimo Roll sequence in his mind; he placed his paddle in the required position, took a deep breath and flipped his kayak over.

Now suspended upside down, Corporal Stupid stayed cool. Sweeping his paddle in an arc he waited for the point when his craft would be in a position to give the final flick of the hip. It didn't. Corporal Stupid remained suspended upside down in the murky brown water. Perhaps one more sweep would do it. It didn't. Time for Plan B.

Plan B was of course, abandon ship, or kayak. All one has to do is pull the cord at the front of the cockpit to release the spray deck, place one's hands at the side and pull yourself out. This is fairly easy manoeuvre and fortunately Captain Stupid was able to perform it without a hitch. He surfaced only to discover the current was taking his kayak one way and his paddle the other. Some five minutes of frantic swimming gathered everything together and he struggled his way to the bank against the flow.

Captain Sensible took over at this point and advised me that a second attempt, although with a possibility of success, probably also included an element of disaster. Drowning also featured in the equation.

My wife was less than impressed when I . . . no it wasn't me, it was Corporal Stupid who related the episode. The fellow just can't keep his mouth shut. I was subsequently ordered to go on a proper course to learn to roll a kayak. If I must.

This I did, with disastrous results. Pushing myself up from the side of the swimming pool with my less than perfect hip flick, I tore the ligaments in my shoulder. Now some three months, umpteen physio sessions and a Cortisone injection later, it still isn't one hundred per cent.

Corporal Stupid has been demoted to Lance Corporal.

Waterhouse.

RANT

Taking a stand on/in dog muck.

You can call it poop if you must. You can also attend to it
with a poop scoop and pop it in a doggy poop bin. But this
attempt to sanitise dog shit doesn't wash with me.

I have a twice-daily parade of dog owners on poo patrol,
hurrying past my house to empty their hounds on a nearby
grassy area (where children play). Why anyone would wish
to spend an hour of every day, acting as a lavatory attendant
to a dog is beyond me. The dogs themselves aren't always
as punctual as their attendants either, and often get caught
short leaving dollops of the stuff on the pavement. Should
you ever confront the owners of these pedigree poo

dispensers, you are the one regarded as the anti-social element.

A couple of weeks ago I berated some chap outside my house, as his attempts to scoop up his dog's rather sloppy output had resulted in him spreading it around the pavement. The fact that he had made this feeble attempt was, in his mind, excuse enough to abandon the residue for me to hose away – or see it spread by foot or car tyre up my drive.

I don't get it. What is it about owning a dog in an urban area? If I lived out in the country I would possibly consider owning one, if I could take it for its essential walks through the fields and woods. Even then, I don't think I could abide walking home swinging a plastic bag filled with doggy doings if it had decided to relieve itself on a footpath. My dog would live where dogs should too – in a kennel.

Not only does dog poo stink, but also dogs themselves can be rather smelly. Homes that have them have a distinct doggy odour. I certainly wouldn't buy a house that was previously home to a dog. The garden would probably be full of canine cack and riddled with toxocara eggs too. Turn a blind eye to that problem and you could end up doing just that!

The real culprits are the night shifts. These sly customers sneak out under cover of darkness to share their smelly, gross product with us. No poop scoops here. These are the ones who turn our pavements into minefields.

With some six million dogs in Britain this amounts to a daily tally of twelve million doggy droppings. That's eighty four million a week. Spread this across the nation (which is basically what they're doing) and consider that some 50% of which must be on our streets.

We're in the shit.

"I think there may be a link here with your ongoing constipation problem."

"Nice header Smiffy!"

The casey, bladder and concrete boots.

Driving around our local Lancashire countryside I find myself pointing out some obscure field or village sports ground and my wife will cut me off before I can utter a word, " I know'" she'll sigh, "You played football there." " Yeh, right," I'll murmur, "Sorry." This is a ritual that has gone on for years, but it's difficult to say nothing. Those were the days when lads battled it out, regardless of the weather in the local leagues, and these fields were the battlegrounds.

As schoolboys in the 40s and 50s, we played under the most dire conditions. The ball itself was a case ball, known as a casey. Descriptive terms in football have always been unimaginative. Case ball – casey, football – footy, goal keeper – goalie and so on. The 'casey' was a ball sewn together from oblong leather panels and with a rubber inflatable bladder. The bladder had a tubular neck about two inches long. It was inflated with a bike pump, then the neck folded over and bound with string. This was then tucked into the case and the whole issue was laced up with a leather thong. I tell you all this to point out that there was no such thing as a round ball. They were round-ish, but all had a bulge where they were laced up. A bulge to be wary of too.

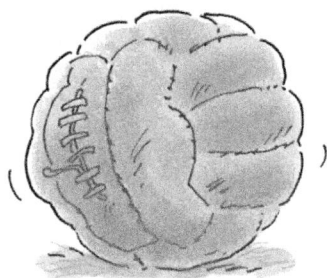

The lethal casey.

Heading the ball always threatened contact with the lace. This could imprint a distinct Frankenstein effect across the forehead. In wet weather, these then increased the risk of concussion. I'm positive that some of the lads from that era sustained the same damage, as do boxers over a period of time. If one of these water-laden balls caught you full on the thigh at speed you were marked for the afternoon with a stinging red image of the case ball's leather panels.

Until I was a teenager, the only football boots on offer were created by someone with obviously no interest or knowledge of football. I'd go so far as to say no idea about boots per se. Nobody ever questioned them for years. They were made from the hardest leather nature could provide, if indeed nature did provide it. Which part of the cow produced anything so inflexible I can't imagine. Even a cow's backside is more supple, otherwise it wouldn't function! It was akin to hardboard. These boots were just long enough at the ankles to ensure that they dug into the flesh and chaffed. They were laced by laces of extraordinary length, which were bound round the foot itself and then around the ankle in a Chinese foot binding exercise. This rendered the foot immovable. Your foot became a club – and was used by some as such. Across the top of the boot was a leather strap, which distinguished the football boot from any other kind of boot, the purpose of which I never discovered. Another ludicrous feature was the toecap. A kind of industrial device, designed to protect the wearer from falling masonry.

The designer of this monstrous foot impediment must have assumed that footballers kick the ball with the toe, despite the 'toe ender' being a common derogatory term for any sub-standard, uncontrolled shot. Then the final act of cruel, pain inducing stupidity – the studs. These were created from little off cut discs of the hardboard/leather about half an inch in diameter and nailed together to stand another half inch. The nails protruded for about a quarter of an inch and were hammered into the sole of the boot. The length of the nails was about equivalent to the thickness of the sole. After a few hours of use, the nails would make their presence felt. Before each game, all over the country, young lads would have to take a hammer to the inside of their boots or use a last to flatten off as many nails as they could. Eventually the business end of the stud would wear away to expose the nail heads. These were the cause of lacerations raked upon generations of young limbs.

Accidental injuries for the most part, but in the hands (or on the feet) of some, these were no less than weapons. Shin pads were an essential item to protect against the afore mentioned boot directed at your shin and aimed with intent. I used to supplement mine with folded up newspaper.

With hindsight, I think the game should have been

regarded, as a dangerous sport. Not just because of the manic behaviour of some of the participants – but based on what we wore. The actual football boot of the era – and the brain damaging, mini medicine ball itself.   The case ball.

—

Printed in Great Britain
by Amazon

30063835R00175